The Bearer
Forgiving As Christ

M. William Ury

The Bearer
Forgiving As Christ
M. William Ury

Copyright © 2015 Teleios Press

Teleios Press
Jackson, Mississippi
Visit our website at www.teleiospress.com

ISBN-10: 1-5120048-5-5
ISBN-13: 978-1-5120048-5-4

Printed in the United States of America

Book Design by Stacey Gaines
Morrison Design & Marketing

First Edition: May 2015
052015

Acknowledgements

I want to thank the wonderful, responsive and vulnerably honest friends who allowed me over the years to share what I was learning from Scripture about the massive doctrine of forgiveness. When I started preaching on this topic I was astounded how many who responded to the message carried large tracts of bitterness in their hearts. Their honesty encouraged me to look inside my own heart and face my own need of gracious release within.

As this project took shape two colleagues encouraged me incessantly. Dr. Steve Blakemore and Dr. Matt Friedeman have shown patient love mixed with constant accountability through the process of writing. They have been friends and co-laborers with me in the Gospel for nearly thirty years.

Stacey Gaines met this novice in the world of publishing and offered expertise, creativity, patience and skill in the production of every part of this book. That she took this project during the arrival of her first baby is a testament to her faithful commitment and servant heart.

My sister, Hope Owsley lovingly critiqued every word of the manuscript. She helped give my words a lucidity they would not have had otherwise.

Others I must thank: Wesley Biblical Seminary for a sabbatical to write these ideas, my youngest sister, Grace Ensz, and my heart-friend, Roe Frazer for reading the manuscript, evangelist and friend Nelson Perdue for interest in this project and for my dear friends Scot Thigpen and Steve Ratcliff, who meeting with me in an accountability group, encouraged me to pursue this project in a way that was one of the greatest expressions of friendship I have ever known. Mary Friedeman gave the text her critical expertise for which I am grateful.

My precious, forbearing and forgiving wife, Diane is the main reason this book has been produced. She has been both lovingly critical and constantly supportive. I have seen the power of the grace of our Savior work in her life in many contexts over thirty years of marriage. No one has benefitted more than me from her heart that bears me in love. What this book points to is the reality she has shown me in actuality.

I praise my Lord and Savior, Jesus Christ for the opportunity to share what I have only begun to learn from a host of others. My Bearer has taken me into Himself, set me free, and I will never be the same.

Pentecost 2015

I would like to dedicate this
book to the man who has most
exemplified the freedom of both
receiving and giving forgiveness
- my father.

William A. Ury (1930-2010)

The Bearer

CHAPTER OUTLINE

> *Then Peter came and said to him, "Lord, how often shall my bother sin against me and I forgive him? Up to seven times?" Jesus said to him, "I do not say to you up to seven times, but up to seventy times seven."*
>
> Matthew 18:21

1

The Lesson of 490

> If there is one thing which is obviously either a part of the universe
> or not – and on knowing whether it is or not our life depends –
> it is the forgiveness of sins.
>
> Charles Williams, *The Forgiveness of Sins*

COULD YOU FORGIVE ME?

I was seventeen years old when I was first introduced to Simon Wiesenthal's famous book *The Sunflower*.[2] It was in those hazy days of trying unsuccessfully to be a hippie that I was thrust into a humanities class of young people who were more focused on their hair length than the intricacies of reality. In my virtually unreflective life the book hit me like a two by four. I did not have the categories to deal with its fundamental issue.

Wiesenthal experienced the terrors of nearly a dozen Nazi prison camps but *The Sunflower* deals with the implications of one particularly excruciating experience. The unique structure of the book allows for the reflections of over thirty scholars from multiple religious traditions and diverse philosophical schools to give responses to the hellish vignette.

In the story Simon Wiesenthal is pulled out of a work detail one morning and led unsuspectingly into an upstairs room of a technical high school which had been converted into a Reserve Hospital. He was concerned because every new job held the inevitable possibilities of humiliation, torture, or doom.

A nurse grabbed him out of the detail and ushered him to a room that held only one patient. She hurried away, and Wiesenthal was left to assess why he was alone with this person. The rustling from the bed became more discernible as a man whose body had been ravaged by a bomb explosion moaned through his bandages. The twenty-one year old soldier was dying a slow, painful death. As Wiesenthal neared the cot he heard the man speaking weakly, yet desperately. The Nazi grabbed the Jewish prisoner's hand and would not let it go for hours as he spun out his guilt-ridden story.

The SS had made life hell for Jews across Europe and intensely so in the death camps. This man was trained to be brutal and merciless, especially to sub-humans like the Jews. Although this dying man had shown signs of sensitivity to the Jews, he told of a day when his platoon of Storm Troopers was given a horrendous order. In the square of a Ukrainian town, a group of Jews had been corralled. Several men from the cowering crowd were forced to take cans of gasoline into a three-story building. Then the rest, men, women and many children, were savagely herded into the house. Other Jews from a truck were crammed in on top of the crowded victims. The door was locked on three hundred Jews.

He recalled that the soldiers were commanded to throw hand grenades through the windows of the building. The ghastly carnage that followed was demonic. Those who died in the inferno were fortunate. Others tried to jump out of the windows. The SS soldier told Weisenthal that he was only acting under orders. But one moment had seared itself indelibly into his soul. He watched one entire family, already aflame, jump only to be mowed down by the rifles he and his platoon had aimed at the house. The dying man could not get that family, especially the face of the young son, out of his head. He could not function. All he could think about was the inexplicable horror expressed in that small, defenseless face. The memory of the boy's expression left him consumed with guilt and shame.

The doomed man's request was based upon a horrific occurrence in which he had been complicit. Perishing now in that military hospital, the soldier confided that the face of that little boy had haunted him every single night. He knew his end was near. He pleaded with Wiesenthal, not knowing if there were any Jews left, for the thing he knew he needed most. That little boy could not absolve him, so in his last moments the guard was grasping for a substitute, a vicarious representative. As his life ebbed away alone in the dark, both physically and spiritually, he asked for what he sought most so that he might have some peace before his end came.

"Could you forgive me for what I did? Please."

Simon Wiesenthal said that in that intense situation he thought hard for a moment. He almost did it. Almost – just to help a man to die peacefully. But he found he could not; he turned on his heels and walked out of the door, leaving the man unforgiven. The soldier died that night.

The intriguing thing about this scenario is that it is followed by scholars and philosophers and theologians asking the simple question: Was Simon right or wrong in what he did? Only a handful determined that Wiesenthal erred on that day decades ago.

If your answer to this moral question comes quickly, I would say you have not carefully thought through the nature of forgiveness.

We all face very difficult ethical and moral tragedies in our lives. All of us do. All of us will. Forgiveness may very well be one of the most difficult things in the world to offer or to receive. Despite the difficulty, there is forgiveness in Jesus Christ which should supersede and inform every other response in our lives and help us understand a just response to evil.

Are we leaving unforgiven people in our lives who need to be freed?

Even harder may be the question: Are we forgiven?

The answer to the latter is directly tied to the first.

***

The Arithmetic of Forgiveness

Most scholars recognize that Matthew purposely positions an important group of teachings prior to Jesus' entering Jerusalem. These immediate "pre-Cross" teachings will become ever more critical in the disciples' thinking as Christ's death approaches.

Earlier in the book of Matthew, Jesus taught on the birthing of the Kingdom of God in a disciple's life (chapter 13). Now, as He transitions to the Cross, He deepens the teaching on that reality by addressing what it truly means to live with His actual Lordship over our lives. What He works in us must be expressed in everyday life.

At the beginning of chapter 18 Jesus says, if you are going to live under my authority, you must be humble toward one another (vv. 1-4). This is absolutely foundational to the teaching of Jesus[3] Without humility nothing else works. One cannot live a moment of the Christian life without humility. Forgiveness is not possible without a humble spirit. Then Christ says, don't put any stumbling block in front of those who are weaker. Don't tempt them; don't do anything to produce evil in their lives. In fact, He says very strongly, if you do, there is real trouble ahead for that self-centered life (vv.5-9).

Next, Jesus turns to another difficult requirement for Kingdom living. He has the audacity to claim that we must be watchful for the brothers or sisters, the sheep, who stray. He does not allow judgment or rejection which are easy expressions of prideful disdain; He undeniably states that if a 'little one' has been lured away by sin, we must show the same concern a Shepherd does for his sheep. Thus, we must leave the secure majority and risk losing everything by going out and showing deep concern for each lost one (vv.10-14).

One can see a pattern in the themes brought together here:

Humility –> Deference –> Seeking the Wayward

Each of these themes is a particular form of relationship that is distinctly King-like in action. They arise out of a poverty of spirit that reflects the self-giving nature of the Savior.

Immediately Jesus moves to a particular form of 'straying.' If there is a person in your fellowship who needs to be reproved or rebuked, you must first go to them personally. If they do not listen to you, then take two or three with you. If the needy one still is hard-hearted, then take the issue before the church.

Now, I'm intrigued that in this context comes the marvelous verse, "For where two or three are gathered together, there I am in the midst" (v.20). We often use that verse in relation to worship, but it is vitally important to realize that Jesus first uses it in a crucial moment of Christian relationship. He wants His lordship to affect our relationships; His desire for us is that we be so deeply unified in the body of Christ that each of us can actually approach somebody, or be approached, for reproof. When that type of critical engagement happens, the most important person involved must be Jesus Christ.

Where two or three are gathered in reproving or being reproved, if anything is going to result besides bitterness and brokenness, He must be there. If He is not present, then any form of reproof can become just another human attempt at power plays which do not set anyone free.

This sensitivity to the community and to the presence of Christ is absolutely crucial when we discuss the possibility of forgiveness. Forgiveness is another form of humility. St. John of the Cross (1542-1591) catches this point exactly when he comments:

> It is noteworthy that he (Jesus) did not say: Where there is one alone, there I am; rather, he said: Where there are at least two. Thus God announces that he does not want the soul to believe only by itself the communications it thinks are of divine origin….God will not bring clarification and confirmation of the truth to the heart of one who is alone.[4]

We cannot live out our life in the King's presence without others. We must both receive and give in community in order for forgiveness to have its full recreating power.

One can see the intensification of Kingdom-relationships in Matthew. The birthing of the Kingdom in our lives produces other-oriented hearts that show humility, deference, watch-care, and mutual admonition. By this time most of us have clicked off. We think to ourselves, "Yeah…right. That's an impossible goal!" But Jesus is not done. There is a constant desire in the Master's heart for us to experience true life in the Light. Refusing His Kingly reign is an invitation to a life of shallow relationship at best. Most of us have settled for much less than shallowness.

At this point in His logic and in His teaching, Jesus moves to forgiveness. This instruction comes out of a deep sense of His lordship over the transformation He has begun in us through the new birth. His life borne in us must issue into the mutuality of the body of Christ. If I am humble, if I am open to making sure my life is not a stumbling block, if I show concern for one who is lost or one who is struggling with temptation, if I am willing to be reproved or to reprove another, then imagine the intimacy that would produce. Then I can talk about forgiveness. The context in this passage (Mt. 18) is extremely important for us to understand. The flow of thought reveals the depth of relationships that is necessary in order for forgiveness to truly occur in a person's life or in the body of Christ. From that setting, we are able to move from the community of believers to the world with our forgiveness.

What happens next is a classic in the annals of "disciple stupidity" and it is an open door for Jesus to proclaim the glory of his marvelous grace. Peter (speaking for most of us) asks a rather interesting question. He queries, "Jesus, how many times do I have to forgive? Seven times seventy?" Why did Peter come up with the number seven? If you research rabbinic literature you will find that the Jewish religious leaders had a number for the extent of longsuffering - three. If a person hurt you three times, the rabbi said, the fourth time you can respond in a way that will get their attention. Nobody should stand under another person's abuse more than three times. It's simply not right. It would be just to respond with vengeance.

I remember a time during my high school years before I was a Christian. One of the greatest thrills of my life was to beat up my younger brother every evening. Thane was a scrawny, lanky teenager and I took great pleasure in making his life miserable night after night just before supper. Oh, the joy of fist upon flesh.

One evening, after a summer of not seeing him much, (which was just fine with me), he showed up. I remember clearly that as he moved across the living room I began to feel the rush of past aggression unrequited for three months. I pushed him against the mantle with a well-placed punch to his chest. This time, however, everything was different. He did not cower in fear. He did not stumble or whine as I had delighted in years previous. I pushed him again.

The rush of power coursed through my veins. Then my tyranny was confronted. After the second shove, he went into a weird, swaying stance that I will never forget. He spread his legs apart and began to tap the toes of his right foot lightly on the floor. Nonchalantly, he spoke, each word enunciated with calm strength. His words etched themselves into my brain. "Bill, you can hit me one more time. But if you touch me a third time, I will kill you." His gaze had a deadly solemnity to it that I had not encountered before.

      I found out later that evening that Thane had been taking karate lessons all summer long. He had learned the art of self defense to prevent any further attacks from me. I must be quick to add that I spent the next couple years of my life taking karate just to protect myself from my brother because he was so good, so deadly in his martial arts acumen.

      Note it well - most religions, like my brother in his karate ethic, have a numbers game going with forgiveness. Forgiveness is hard. Sometimes it feels impossible. So, to assuage our consciences, we set a number as a moral boundary. We say three or four offenses, so that Buddhist monks or Jewish Rabbis trying to be patient can get a grip on a realistic standard.[5] If you think about it, Peter is attempting an impressive spiritual feat. He is offering more than most people would give a person who sins against them. He has walked with Incarnate Love; he has watched Jesus forgive, so he has done some pretty impressive computing, compared to most religions. "Well, I'll double the normal bottom line for forgiveness and add one for good measure." One has to wonder if he smiled as he enunciated the number seven which bore so much meaning for anyone who knew the God of the Old Testament.[6] It is almost a gambling configuration. "I'll see your rule; I will double the number and ante up one more. Lord, is that not impressive?"[7]

      Peter saw himself as super-spiritual, just like most of us would have done in his situation. That is, if we are satisfied to reduce forgiveness to an issue of numbers. How easily we impress ourselves with our calculated forbearance.

In the early years of my marriage I wondered if something like this was necessary. There was a kind of mental book that I kept when my wife didn't do exactly what I thought she should do. I was so self-centered and immature that I considered almost anything a "sin" against me. I was a master counter and the numbers grew. But in my heart I knew that this was really the story of my own spiritual ineptitude, keeping a ledger against my own precious wife.

Paul had something to say about this in I Corinthians 13:5 when he says that one thing which *agape* love evidences clearly to other people is that it "keeps no account of wrongs." The Greek word for 'account' there actually means a ledger, a book.

Little Black Books

I grew up on the tropical island of Taiwan and the only air-conditioned room in the house was my parents' bedroom, which also served as my dad's office. I remember vividly the neatness of my father's meticulous library. Every shelf had just the number of books to leave space for a knickknack. The books descended perfectly from larger to smaller size on each shelf. I spent a lot of time in the office trying to escape the sweltering heat, and it was there I discovered the book *Games People Play*.[8] I was intrigued by the title, though I had no idea what the book was about. But as I leafed through the chapters, I distinctly remember the chapter in which the author discussed keeping trading stamps.

There was a day, even for a missionary kid thousands of miles from American shores, when we all kept books of stamps. From the grocery store to the tops of cereal boxes we cut and pasted those things into small books with religious fervor. In *Games People Play*, Eric Berne compares "trading stamps" to how some people build relationships.

There is a record-keeping mentality that justifies itself when people do us wrong, and we don't retaliate because we want to at least keep up the appearance of civility.

The author argued that we all keep emotional green stamps. We mark the issue that is a 'sin' done against us. And we paste that experience in our heart. We keep those lists and gather and paste them in that inner "book" and at just the right moment – we redeem them. We are artists at that moment. Just when the person who has been hurting us or doing something wrong to us is the weakest and their jugular is exposed, we cash in.

That vindictive mentality, or rather heart orientation, is almost universally true. I am proof; husbands can become artists at it. Wives can become artists at it. We know exactly how and when to get back at that loved one when they are at their most vulnerable point. We bring up all the self-satisfying backlog of wrongs done, and with self-righteous indignation we put our spouses in their place. I began to be a lot less critical of Peter because I realized there were long account books in my heart against the people I loved most. They were full of ledgers of emotional green stamps I had pasted in there, and I was waiting for the right time to redeem my emotional payback book on those who 'deserved' it. Little black books, kept religiously, are the death knell to intimacy and wholeness in relationships.

What would it mean for a person to walk through life unforgiving and unforgiven? If you are unforgiven, then you can't forgive anyone else, and you spend your life trying to shoot people down in a hopeless attempt to bring meaning to your life. Somewhere there's got to be a stop to it. Apparently, Jesus is saying on His way to the pivot in his ministry which will take him to Jerusalem and the Cross, that we have to understand that, "To live in My Kingdom, My absolute authority must be over every facet of your life. You must be humble and other-oriented with a forgiving spirit if you are to know the fullness that is the inheritance I offer you."

My hunch is that if we were truly honest we would admit that we live in the Christian church among families with a low-grade fever of retributive justice. We thus discount the Spirit of Jesus in our lives. His authority is unrecognized in the library of little green books, tattered from overuse.

It is almost humorous that Peter asks about how often he should forgive his sinful brother. The question ought to be the opposite. How often should my brother or sister forgive me? We always are keen on judgment and justice when we are the recipients of a transgression. I have often thought about who Peter looked at in the group when he said, "My brother." Was it Matthew? Or Judas? Maybe John.

When Peter heard Jesus speak on forgiveness he moved to his lifetime default position that could be justified by contrasting it with the best religion the world had ever known. He quickly made it a numbers issue and Jesus said *"Peter, forgiveness is not a numbers game."* It is about relationships and what makes deep, true and clean relationships possible. Our question is, what enables relationship? We want to encourage it. Deepen it. Experience it at the deepest levels possible. But if we forgive with a number attached to it, then we discount Him and His awesome grace.

We easily fall into the trap of Peter's perception on forgiveness. C.S. Lewis once stated that even if it were possible to forgive a person's sin 490 times, what would we do if God called us to forgive the *same* sin committed against us 490 times?[9]

That's a different thing. That is where every little black book is revealed.

In a parallel passage in Luke 17:4, Jesus commands us to forgive the sinning brother even if he sins against us and repents seven times a day. What if we were to take Lewis' striking statements to heart before our typical reaction of a list of reservations? What if the first response was to forgive and not to grab for our ledger?

I can forgive if it's for a lot of different situations, but what if it's the same wrong done to me over and over again? Of course, Jesus is not teaching that we must forgive murder or other forms of heinous evil seven times a day.[10] Nor is he saying that sin does not have serious consequences even if forgiven. He is talking about real relationships between real people broken by sin, and that is always a threat to our sense of right. I believe that's the place where most of us keep accounts, and we keep them assiduously deep in our hearts.

One of my mentors during college referred to people like this as spiritual and emotional debt collectors. In a warped way we have our own form of becoming spiritual repo men, reclaiming what we think is ours. Later on in the business of tit for tat, when somebody can't come up with the right amount of money or the right amount of love to respond to us, we move in for the take down. We take what we rightfully deserve. We give to the person involved exactly what they've got coming.

But could I forgive the way Jesus calls me to forgive?

A few years ago a friend was in the middle of a period of counseling and of deep heart searching. In the midst of the pain a book was recommended by Robert Magee called *The Search for Significance*. The chapter in that book on forgiving others exposed many typical excuses for explaining away the call to radical forgiveness. We can become experts at rationalizing ledgers of bitter unforgiveness. Let me paraphrase here:

- The offense was too great. I can forgive small things but that infraction was too large.

- Why should I forgive that person who will never accept the responsibility for the offense?

- They've got to know what they did to me and not do it to anyone else.

- I'd like to forgive, but that person isn't really, truly sorry.

- The person involved never asked for forgiveness.

- I'd forgive but it's just going to be meaningless. It's cheap forgiveness. Isn't forgiveness supposed to change them?

- I just don't like the person. If I forgive, that means I've got to like them.

- I'll be a hypocrite if I forgive because I just don't feel like it and I want to be honest. Hypocrites do what they don't feel like and, therefore, I'm not going to forgive.

- I'll forgive but I'll never ever forget.[11]

The list goes on. But doesn't this reveal where most of us live? That ought to break our hearts, especially since there is someone who has your face before them as they make those exemptions. We are so excuse-laden and numbers-oriented that our relationships show it. We lack a forgiving spirit and what that really is all about. We testify that Jesus has birthed in us a life that is so transforming that we claim to want to walk in His ways. Oh, really? How many black books of numbers do we carry around in the breast pocket of our self-protection?

The Spirit of Christ alone can enable the forgiveness that sets people free.

DEFINITION OF FORGIVENESS

I want to offer a working definition of forgiveness. Provisionally it will be brief in order to get the themes before us. We will keep looking at its meaning and keep tweaking it as we go along. It comes from various sources and my own experience. Years of my own failures, as well as watching the chaos of unforgiveness in other lives, has helped me when I find myself in a distressing relationship. I may not be able to discern what 'sin' against me looks like all the time, but I need to be engaged with all that I know of Jesus in every situation. So I begin to think along these lines when I have been wronged, used, humiliated, or slandered. As one who is a committed Christian this 'definition' may not sound as theological as some but it is based upon biblical, theological and experiential realities.[12]

Forgiveness is a:

- *Process:* that is a real, on-going relational process. This process starts with me, in my own person, as the wronged one. This does not exclude the fact of my sense of being wronged from God's perspective on the sin and its ultimate judgment.[13] Forgiving is also a,

- *Bearing:* I have to bear the wrong-doer in my heart. I must put to death my sense of justice, any moral barrier I have against releasing the sinning one from what they deserve. And forgiveness is an,

- *Openness:* Which means (and this might be withering to some of us) that I must be willing to open the possibility of the relationship once again.

Keep reading. It is going to be difficult for most of us. There is always something in our lives which we can rationalize as unforgivable. In the next few chapters we'll be unpacking what forgiveness means. Every single word has been chosen very carefully because we don't want to promote a wrong understanding of forgiveness, such as, excusing sin.

This difficult process must begin with my entire person. The areas which need the most attention in this painful process are the mind, the heart and one's attitude as a wronged person. But it must include a radical judgment of my own nature and character. I have to face what is actually happening and only the Holy Spirit can make that clear. We will come to this issue in a later chapter.

Forgiveness is always moral. But before we categorize the types of forgiveness we need to comprehend and embrace God's best for us in the divine gift of forgiveness from the heart. At base we have to confront this issue. If we are truly disciples of Jesus, with His Life breaking forth into and out of our own, then we cannot limit forgiveness. As someone has said in comparing our need to be forgiven with those around us who need the same, "If there is a limit to forgiveness, none of us would be disciples."

The Bible repeatedly says that we must forgive to be forgiven. In Matthew 18, the Lord uses an unnerving number, 490, to cause us to cast our futile attempts at forgiveness at His feet. By that impossible requirement He is transcending any small numbers game we might try to construct in our fallen relationships. There is a deeper lesson to that impossible number. It points to a Spirit-filled life and will that keeps on forgiving.

In our lifetime, there may be a few who come to us with a desire to initiate the exacting, but freeing, discipline of forgiveness. Many others will never seek to offer repentance, much less forgiveness. But we can still be free of the heavy weight of a numbers approach as we live out of a grace-based forgiveness.[14] Jesus says we can set people free and in that remarkable spiritual alchemy we can be set free ourselves in ways we never anticipated.

There is great hope in that.

---

[1] All references are taken from the New American Standard Bible (Nashville: Thomas Nelson, 1978) unless translated by the author or another translation is used and noted in the text.

[2] Simon Wiesenthal, *The Sunflower: with a Symposium* (New York: Shocken Books, 1976). This is a profoundly influential book in the area of forgiveness. The full story (7-79) is followed by 31 responses (83- 172). Several of the authors that I have read spend significant time on this book for good reason. See L. Gregory Jones *Embodying Forgiveness: A Theological Analysis* (Grand Rapids: Eerdmans, 1995), 281-290. I remember hearing Ravi Zacharias say once that Philip Yancey's article on forgiveness, which starts out with the Wiesenthal story, which appeared in the November 22, 1985 edition of Christianity Today, was one of the most profound reflections he had ever read on the subject. I would concur. It is also intriguing to note how many writers on forgiveness turn to the Holocaust as a source for reflection. Probably the most famous statement on the absence, or silence or eclipse, of God for a Jew living through the horror is Elie Weisel's *Night* (New York: Hill and Wang, 2006) esp. pp.64-65. I have found scores of stories in my research that show the indelible mark which that 20th century catastrophe has left on theological reflection until today. For a Jewish perspective that is a challenging critique of Christian theology regarding the Holocaust see, Irving Greenberg "Cloud of Smoke and Pillar of Fire," in *Holocaust: Religious and Philosophical Implications* (St. Paul, MN: Paragon House, 1989), 305-345. There is no sustained discussion of forgiveness in this book. The influential work by Viktor Frankl, *Man's Search for Meaning* (Boston: Beacon Press, (1959) 2006 ed.), is more theologically hopeful but it also does not deal with forgiveness at any level.

[3] Stanley Hauerwas, *Matthew* (Grand Rapids: Brazos, 2006), 160-167 underscores the centrality of humility in the successive paragraphs of chapter 18. He interprets Peter's rebuke of Jesus (apparently referring to 16:22) as the fear that Jesus' repeated references to his own death was a humiliating self-deprecation. For Hauerwas humility is 'the name rightly given to the recognition of our sins,' as disciples we must 'learn how to break back into' humility, and it is only present in a community where there is 'no pretense' *Ibid.*, 162.

[4] St. John of the Cross *The Collected Works of St. John of the Cross* trans. K. Kavanaugh and O. Rodriguez (Washington D.C.: Institute of Carmelites Studies Publications, 1991), 234.

[5] Charles Talbert, *Matthew* (Grand Rapids: Baker Academic, 2010) , 223 offers a couple of instances from Talmudic literature. One, *Avot R. Nat 40* deals with the idea that God will not forgive a fourth time the recalcitrant sinner which adds to the pathos of our present passage. Others support the limit of three offenses *b. Yoma,86b* and *t. Yoma 4:1.*

[6] It is significant that the numbers, "seven" and "seventy seven" show up together in Gen 4:24. At the beginning of civilization after the Fall and the murder of his brother Abel, Cain and his progeny are identified by vengeance. One wonders if this dawned on Peter. We can be sure that it did not escape the mind of Jesus as he offered an entirely different ethic. Robert Mulholland has uncovered this underlying vengeful spirit as a fundamental sin in connection to the 'city' in his insightful theological commentary *Revelation (Grand Rapids: Zondervan, 1990)*. Some (cf. Hauerwas, *Matthew* p. 166) have also tied the number seventy-seven to the adumbration of Lev 25:8-17 and the sabbatical year. The year of Jubilee included the liberation of those enslaved by debt being one of the categories which Jesus elevates to the level of grace by His divine being and ministry.

[7] Chrysostom refers to the number seven as one indication of many or without limit, Saint Chrysostom, *Homilies on the Gospel of St. Matthew*, Nicene and Post-Nicene Fathers,(hereafter NPNF) Series I:Vol 10, (1888 ed.), 376. Augustine, in the same vein

as our discussion asks rhetorically what if a brother sins seventy-eight times, would retribution be fitting then? *Sermon* 33:3, NPNF Series I: Vol. 6, (1888 ed.), 363

[8] Eric Berne, *Games People Play* (New York: Grove Press, 1964). Augustine mentions the connection of the numbers in the discussion with Peter and the seventy seven and the generations from Christ to Adam in Matt 1:1-16. Augustine, Sermon 33:5-6 in NPNF Series I:Vol. 6, 1888 ed., 364.

[9] C.S. Lewis, *Reflections on the Psalms* (San Diego: Harcourt:, 1986), 25. The preceding idea is also helpful here, "There is no use in talking as if forgiveness were easy. We all know the old joke, "You've given up smoking once: I've given it up a dozen times." In the same way I could say of a certain man, "Have I forgiven him for what he did that day? I've forgiven him more times than I can count: For we find that the work of forgiveness has to be done over and over again." (Ibid, 24-25).

[10] There are other sources which categorize the various types of both divine and human forgiveness. Our purpose here is to focus on the central meaning and application of forgiveness. The theological background of all interpreters of forgiveness can be seen very quickly as is discernible in this brief treatise.

[11] Robert McGee *The Search for Significance* (Houston, TX: Rapha Publishing, 1990), pp. 313-321. Interestingly, at the end of the chapter McGee offers a series of reflective questions on a scriptural passage of forgiveness – Matt 18:21-35. I saw a quote recently that stung me. It went something like this; 'Men forget but don't forgive. Women forgive but don't forget.'

[12] I began thinking and preaching about forgiveness long before L. Gregory Jones' *Embodying Forgiveness: A Theological Analysis* appeared. His critique (primarily found in pp.35-70) of what he terms the 'therapeutic' school of thought regarding forgiveness continues to reverberate through much of the evangelical discussion of forgiveness. I mention that here to make the reader aware that I am not desirous to make forgiveness an individual matter at all. But there must be a starting point for the process. I cannot be sure that the 'other' will ever seek to be reconciled. Nor can I be sure that the 'church' and its 'habits' and 'practices of holiness in communion' will be adequate in the typical situation to mediate to the parties involved what each is responsible for. I strongly agree with Jones on the need to face all self-deception, as well as, admit my need for forgiveness in any way in which I am aiding or abetting any 'other' by complicity in culturally-acceptable sins. This book is not meant to be a full theological response to Jones or to those he criticizes. I hope to offer a helpful analysis for the 'regular' person who is struggling with forgiveness – either in giving it or receiving it. It may be that there is a middle ground between the authors Jones is perturbed with and his more theological assessment.

[13] I started this book on sabbatical leave from the seminary where I had taught for over 23 years. My wife and I made the transition to pastoral ministry and I was under the delusion that I would have time to write in the pastorate! Now several years later, and I hope a bit wiser, I have now read and experienced issues that relate to forgiveness at nearly every sector of life. There are many books I would like to critique and interact with but that must wait for another time. One issue that this 'therapeutic' moniker has raised pertains to whether or not a person can forgive if the offender does not go through the stages of confession and repentance. I hope in what follows the reader will see that I understand that true forgiveness in its most robust sense can only occur if the sinner and sinned against can work through the process of forgiveness. I have found help along these lines in Andy Johnson's *The End of Conflict: Resisting False Utopia in Hope of True Restoration* (n.p.: Restoration Publishing, 2013). Johnson, like L. Gregory Jones is very keen on keeping a clear-headed approach to forgiveness. In his summation Johnson distinguishes biblical forgiveness from the 'therapeutic' school of thought. The former is always relational, Christocentric, other-oriented, and conditional upon the process of forgiveness, *Ibid.*, 283-289. I may not be as critical, nor as insightful, of the therapeutic as these authors but I pray that what follows is not interpreted as unbiblical, introspective, unconditionally oppressive to the offended, and not related to the Savior or His glory. To forgive from the heart means that it must come through the heart of God in Christ and it must be a forgiveness that extends to at least two persons who desire hearts free of all self-centeredness.

He was despised and rejected by men; a man of sorrows, and acquainted with grief; and as one from whom men hide their faces he was despised, and we esteemed him not. Surely he has borne our griefs and carried our sorrows; yet we esteemed him stricken, smitten by God, and afflicted. But he was wounded for our transgressions; he was crushed for our iniquities; upon him was the chastisement that brought us peace, and with his stripes we are healed. All we like sheep have gone astray; we have turned--every-one--to his own way; and the LORD has laid on him the iniquity of us all.

Isaiah 53:3-6

2

Forgiving as Bearing

Everyone says forgiveness is a lovely idea, until they have
something to forgive.

C.S Lewis, *Mere Christianity*

WHY DID THEY ALL HAVE TO DIE?

There are few who would disagree that the idea of forgiveness
that Peter espoused wasdrawn from the Old Testament. He was a
righteous man well aware of the system of substitution that was at the
center of the Israelite faith. If there was sin, there had to be atonement.
No human being could bear sin or atone for it. There had to be another,
someone or something, to take what they deserved.

I remember once looking into the tear-filled eyes of a friend
who is a thoroughgoing animal lover as she pushed me with the
question, "Why did all those animals have to die?" I had never thought
of it before but I immediately began a sort of mental arithmetic.

The time period from Abraham to the Fall of Jerusalem was about 2000 years; the sacrificial system was in place for nearly 1400 years. If one added up the daily sacrifices commanded by the Lord, accompanied by the free-will offerings of Israel, the number would quickly add up to millions of animals. That is a lot of blood; a lot of death. Was Israel merely mimicking other pagan cultures with disregard for the authority of God's voice? Or was there something deeper? Is there something here more central to the nature of reality?

It might be possible that the solution to our sin problem had to be seen in stark relief. The Lord knew that we would never understand the meaning of the Blood without witnessing the carnage that sin produces. Like the anguish of my friend, except to an eternal degree, is the pain in the heart of God over the chaos we invite into our own hearts. Only when we truly see our self-imposed abyss, are we ever really aware of the grandeur of an all-sufficient Deliverer.

A concept of forgiveness like Peter's, and like my friend's, can too easily turn into a focus on the means of forgiveness; it's economy, rather than the deeper sense of meaning that it reveals. We are masters at turning all of salvation into a numbers game. But the Bible forces us to confront that issue just as Jesus did with Peter.

Pictures of True Forgiveness

Forgiveness is only a part of a much larger, grand doctrine of salvation. The many metaphors, or pictures, of what it means to be truly saved have been explored and explained by numerous scholars. The point here is to try to discern the central meaning of the concept of grace that deals with God's holiness and our sinfulness, and how the two natures come together through forgiveness. It is always a mistake to separate one aspect of saving grace from all the others (i.e., redemption, recreation, deliverance, etc.). But it is not wrong to focus on one aspect in order to see it more clearly in relation to the whole panoply of God's self-giving love.

The major terms from which we gain our best concepts regarding forgiveness are as follows: In the Hebrew language we have:

1. *Salah*   Ex. 34:9   forgive, pardon used only of God toward humanity

2. *Kaphar*   Ex. 32:20   to cover, hide, ransom symbol of innocent life to atone given for a guilty party

3. *Nasah*   Ex. 32:7   to lift up, bear, term is used as divine attribute

In Greek there are several major words;

1. *Aphiemi*   Mk 2:7   to send away, to let go, cancel, lit. to send from

2. *Aphesis*   Mk 1:4   remission, deliverance, pardon

3. *Paresis*   Rom 3:5   passing over, expiation, from verb 'to let pass', 'to allow'

4. *Charizomai* Col 2:13   to offer grace, to remit, to give pardon[1]

The sheer amount of passages and the diversity of interpretations of their meaning in relation to the topic of forgiveness can be overwhelming. But we need to focus on the most crucial questions. What does forgiveness mean? How does God forgive? It is intriguing that when Jesus looks upon the paralytic and sees the faith of His friends, He looks beyond the outward malady and zeroes in on the deepest need borne within the heart of the man on the pallet. Jesus says, "My son, your sins are forgiven." And the theological teachers began their criticisms with an ironic but unknowing double entendre, "Who can forgive sins but God alone?" (Mk 2:3-12)

Jesus was offering what no lamb slaughtered on the altar of Israel could. It is only in the heart of God incarnate that the burden of human sin and the holiness of God could effectively meet. As Jesus pronounced forgiveness, the shadow of his own cross went over that scene.[2] Everything before Jesus was symbol – pointing to the reality of the self-sacrificing Lamb. Let's look at one of these symbols more deeply.

A Diminished Gospel

The tendency in most modern theology has been to see salvation in terms that predominantly focus on the power of God. If sovereignty is taken as the foundational essence of God, then it is not surprising that our themes will make forgiveness something a transcendent Authority will accomplish. Granted, God is the Forgiver. It is His power, His righteousness, His glory that is at work when rebels, like us, are offered release from condemnation. But that wonderful truth must be held in balance with the coming of the Lamb of God. God did not forgive from Heaven alone. As we said, no drop of blood falling from the altar of the Temple atoned for one sin in itself. Those rituals pointed to the heart of our Redeeming God, Father, Son and Holy Spirit. The forgiveness of Jesus surely issued from His eternal power, but it was (and is) a power that is revealed through self-giving and thus, holy love.

Part of the problem with our gospel in the Western world is that we have diminished the meaning of forgiveness. Rather than participating with joy in the banqueting table of God's gracious nature imparted to all sinners who trust in Him, we have turned repentance into a paganized form of ritualism. We have made forgiveness a mechanical thing – a numbers game.

We have communicated that when God forgives He sends something away. He sends away the consequences, the guilt, and the shame. But something also has to happen to the sin. To forgive is more than a divine declaration of dismissal.

We would lessen everything about Israel's faith and the Incarnation of the Savior if that was all that it took to free us from sins. If we reduce forgiveness merely to divine fiat, characterizing forgiveness only as a statement from God, like when He spoke creation into existence, then there is really no ultimate reason for the Incarnation or the Cross. The major work would have already been done long before Jesus first called Israel to repent.

Most of us pull away from this idea when pushed to consider it. We want more than legal declarations or mere transactions. The lack of ethics within the so-called forgiven Church is an indication of faulty theology. We desire more than a courtroom statement that translates into lives free of guilt, shame and moral laxity. Rather than delving into the deeper meaning of forgiveness, we have tended to settle for simplistic thinking which has produced great harm. Our preoccupation with freedom from the consequences of our sin without an equal emphasis on gaining victory over sin has hamstrung any power we might have had to truly experience and witness to the Gospel.

Protestantism, which began in part out of a reaction to the misuse of ecclesiastical activities for acquiring salvation, has now come full circle. Just like any uninformed Catholic, millions of Protestants sin with various levels of alacrity day after day and they come to a new form of penance: tithing more, attending more, going to an altar repeatedly in order that they might be 'forgiven' - again and again. If you do not believe what I am saying, then take a look at the general lifestyle of most American Protestant Christians. We have diminished forgiveness by emphasizing God's power and depreciating the personal holiness of the human heart which His saving power desires to produce. We have lost a vision for God's desire to make us and keep us new creations.

If our doctrine of divine power is to be rectified it must be done so by incorporating a full doctrine of Jesus Christ as the Lamb of God from the very "foundation of the world" (Rev 13:8). He is the

Only Lamb who "takes away the sin of the world" (Jn 1:29). John uses a word (*airon*) which means 'to lift up' or 'to bear away'. Most references that include that word carry the actual meaning of taking something and putting it in another place. John envisions Jesus doing something that no one else could ever accomplish. The Lamb of God has come to actually bear the full meaning of our rejection of God. By bearing it He will remove it from us and carry it until it has been defeated. We are saved through the divine power which was fully revealed upon the Cross in the One who died there.

When we begin to grasp the magnitude of the substitution of His life *for* ours in order that His Life can *become* ours, then forgiveness begins to contain the meaning that the symbols merely pointed to.[3] Forgiveness is not something done to me, but forgiveness is something which first occurs in the very being of God.

The God Who Bears

I had the privilege of being an assistant to a great man of God for about a year. Dr. Dennis Kinlaw, the former president of Asbury College (now University) was gracious enough to take an immature first-year seminarian into his home and his life. The notes that I took of our conversations while we traveled, drank coffee in foreign airports, ate in truck stops and sat in cramped motel rooms will be priceless treasures all of my life.

Early in our time together he asked me if I had read any of the works of Charles Williams. I can still remember the creeping crimson of shame that crawled up my neck as I saw his very loving but pained reaction to my evident lack of knowledge of this 20th century literary giant and theological mind. It was there that I was introduced to the idea of 'exchange'.

As one of the Inklings (a literary club frequented by C. S. Lewis, J.R.R. Tolkein, and Dorothy Sayers) he has a mysterious edge and a vocabulary to match that can leave the impatient reader undone.

Throughout Williams' works there is the underlying conception of reality based on the idea that in Jesus Christ an exchange has taken place that is the foundation of all true Life. In order for redemption to occur two kinds of life must meet: the supernatural (or spiritual) and the natural. The pride that resulted in the Fall and a destroyed relationship with God means that our natural beings are perverted through and through. But in a glorious exchange, one that begins in time with the Incarnation, Jesus has taken into Himself all of my sin and perversion, and has, in return, given me all of Himself. The method of forgiveness comes second to this. We must fight the numbering tendency and the mechanism of "churchianity". That is something that cuts at the very center of reality.

At one point, Williams simply quotes a large portion of Isaiah's prophecy about the Suffering Servant in chapter 53.[4] Much like what was alluded to above there is no rigorous theological exposition in the Old Testament of the forgiveness offered here, but what we do see are symbols that provide a picture of the Forgiver as one who takes our sins upon Himself:

> *Surely he hath **borne** our griefs*
> *And he has **carried** our sorrows*
> *He was **wounded for** our transgressions*
> *The chastisement of our peace **was upon Him***
> ***With His stripes** we are healed*
> *The Lord **hath laid on Him** the iniquity of us all*
> *As **He will bear** their iniquities*
> *He **bore** the sins of many away.*

Clearly, the recurrent refrain here is that the Chosen One is bearing for others what they could not bear. Everything that sin is and that sin produces has been transferred to a willing, vicarious Substitute – our Bearer - who takes our place in this wondrous exchange which is nothing short of the glory of God revealed.[5] Williams (and my dear friend Dennis Kinlaw) is unable to get very far from this. We, too, need to place this understanding at the center of our lives.

Every year I taught the History of Christian Thought I had my students read a classic by Williams, *The Descent of the Dove*.[6] I think that was the first book Kinlaw thrust into my hands after that initial embarrassing conversation exposing my ignorance. Throughout Williams' artistic and deeply spiritual assessment of the work of the Spirit, which for him is the meaning of the Church's history, there is that theme of exchange. Until the Church realizes that the Spirit of Jesus can make Himself fully known in our flesh, because of what the incarnate Son bore on our behalf, we can never really understand salvation sufficiently to live in freedom from constant guilt.

I will never forget the day that Dr. Kinlaw took the text of Isaiah 53 in Hebrew and worked through a couple of verses with me. He spoke of that work foreseen in the prophet's vision of the 'exchange of redemption' in 53:4. We came to the gripping statement, "Surely he hath borne our griefs." I had studied many of the terms for salvation but we explored the implications of what it meant to bear sin away for another. As he continued my pen dropped to my tablet. I was stunned and forever changed by the Spirit's teaching.

As my beloved friend leaned toward me he said, "Bill, there is another term that elucidates the word 'borne'. It occurs in 53:6, the one we have all memorized. "All we like sheep have gone astray, we have turned everyone to his own way, and the Lord has laid on Him the iniquity of us all." In his inimitable style Dr. Kinlaw chuckled (which meant get ready for your mind to be blown) and said, "The phrase 'laid on him' is unique with a grammatical form which bears unimaginable truth." He went on to describe the grandeur of forgiveness in a way that I had never heard, or if I had, I had never comprehended until that day. "You see," he said, "that verb literally means 'it comes together in him.' All of our sin, our griefs, and the residual damage of them all meet within Him. And when they meet in that One we are delivered; we are set free to be what He made us to be."[7]

I don't remember how I got to my room. All I know is that when I stumbled in and shut the door I began to weep. I had never been so grateful for that word, "forgiveness". Like so many of us I had taken the word too lightly, too glibly, unaware of its grandeur and extensiveness. I had begun to drink of the depth of salvation that He is - not just what He has done. He set me free, He pardoned, He sent away all that threatened my love relationship with Him because He allowed all that I had done to myself that produced grief, both in me and my Savior, to meet in Himself. And in that personal transaction, that glorious exchange, something changed in both of us. I was included in Him and my life became a place where He could live His Life in me.

After the Courtroom

My life has evidenced a radical transformation. For eighteen years I was sort of a mindless adherent to Christianity. Mine was a classic case of "coattails religion." The last three years of that time were a confusing mix of a false front with a seething cauldron of rebellion underneath. And now? All I used to despise I now love. I love gospel preaching. I love churches. It's weird how much I love to go into any church. I love the pews, the pulpits, the spartan Sunday school rooms; I even love the smells of worn carpet and aged hymnals. I especially love altars. I come from a tradition that has incorporated the symbol of kneeling at the 'altar' for a variety of reasons. One of the most beautiful occurrences is when a person finds the forgiveness of Jesus at an altar.

But I have found that unless a person truly explores the mysterious beauty of that forgiveness, they can soon slip into a 'mercantilistic' religiosity. By that I mean a relationship that resembles a business transaction: I offer a prayer of repentance and out comes my pre-paid and packaged forgiveness which I pick up (often at the same altar) again. When I have the privilege of praying with someone at an altar I often find myself speaking too much, but it is only because I want to clarify the meaning of forgiveness and I don't want that person to misunderstand it. What I often hear are deeply self-revealing testimonies cast in courtroom language; pardoned, acquitted, declared righteous; all of which are correct, but not complete in themselves.

I have lived far too long with the courtroom motif, and the transaction mode, which do not hold up under the scrutiny of Scripture, the Spirit's work, or full and vibrant Christian experience. To stay in the courtroom too long places a shadow over the entire Christian mind and heart; it produces a reserve which limits a full-orbed view of forgiveness.

All of this goes back to one of the earlier words we looked at to render a true definition of forgiveness – "to bear." After slaughtering his own brother, Cain cries out even before sin is defined, "My fault (or punishment) is too great to bear" (Gen 4:13). Only the person who has sensed his own sin to that measure can begin to appreciate Another coming to lift that insufferable load.

Symbolically, Israel's high priest bore the people upon his shoulders, his breast and his forehead (Ex. 28:21, 29, 38) as promises of the much deeper identifying work of our Great High Priest. Jesus Christ would do more than an external work or a vocal intercession on behalf of others. He would open Himself to an internal 'bearing' that would define all intercession in a different key.

BEARING

Looking at all the references to nasah (to bear) it seems as if our Forgiver is teaching us something of Himself throughout the old covenant. The term "to bear" logically entails the lifting of an object, then a carrying, and finally a removal or releasing of that which has been borne.[8]

Our family still owns a videotape of an animated version of *Pilgrim's Progress*. We watched that thing so many hundreds of times that we wore out the video. Our girls memorized most of it. When our oldest daughter, JoAnna, was two she called it "Pilgwim's Pwobwems." And that is what they were. If you know the classic tale, Christian carries a huge, heavy load on his back. Nothing can release him until he comes to the foot of the Cross. And there the transaction is made and that unwieldy weight of sin is released from his back and falls into a large cavern. We would often jump up and down and clap at that point in the movie. I actually remember tearing up a time or two when it dawned on me that that is exactly what happened for all of us who have experienced the forgiving grace of Jesus. The one thing not made clear is that the burden was transferred to the heart of our Sin-Bearer. Someone had to bear the burden. And only One did. The One on the Cross, He took our sin and the abyss into Himself and expunged it there in His self-giving love.

With this theme in mind it seems that every action of Golgotha was allowed by the Lamb. He lifted, carried, bore, exchanged, released – forgave. Jesus fulfilled all that His priestly, bearing heart had to, in order to completely receive all that I am, in order that I might become fully pardoned, and that I in turn might become the bearer of the saving Life He is.

Peter was totally unaware of the true Messiah that stood before him at Caesarea Philippi. He was looking for an authority that would fix political agendas. Likewise, we have our own form of misunderstandings when it comes to the Messiah's work. Too often it is exclusively an outward work, something done for us. When in reality the true work is internal. Forgiveness is not a spiritual body shop, a fix-me-up affair; it is a transformational reality that restores me to full relationship with God and my neighbor.[9]

Forgiveness Begins in the Heart of the Triune God

Forgiveness begins in the heart of God. It is borne by the Son of God. Forgiveness must begin in the heart of one who loves the sinner more than himself. It is an "inclusion" (to use another ubiquitous term from Williams) of Another in me. To bear one who is in sin is the experience of many a parent for a wayward child. And I have heard many redeemed sons and daughters (I among them) who attribute their salvation to that earthly bearing which signifies a divine 'bearing'. When it begins to occupy my spiritual attention that I have been included in the most personal of ways in the heart of the Triune God, then forgiveness begins to take on the beauty it is meant to initiate.

I have often thought of the tear stains on the couch in the living room of that Taiwanese parsonage that were products of my recalcitrant and selfish antics. When I would leave for whatever aimlessness sin produced, my own mother would drop to her knees. And often, when I arrived home, she would get up, not having moved since my departure and go back to her bedroom without a word. Sometimes I would look at those stains in utter disgust. What did they mean? What good would they do? Let me tell what good. They were my salvation because they represented a heart that bore a rebel in the midst of his own spiritual death. They shall ever be to me the picture of the reality of my Savior who lived, prayed, suffered and died to bear me in Himself so that I might be able one day to receive that forgiving, transforming grace. God's bearing Heart always precedes that inclusion which is carried in the heart of anyone who intercedes for one they love.

A Personalizing Act

I remember reading about E. Stanley Jones' sanctification experience. It occurred when the Jones realized that he kept dealing with issues that arose from, what he referred to, as the 'cellar' of his life. After a long time of contest with the Spirit of Jesus, there was a sudden discernment of truth in the intrepid young unbeliever. What followed may sound simplistic but it is not to any who have come to understand the glorious exchange. Jones said, "Do you mean that you will take all of my stuff – this junk, this damage, this putrid mess and in return give me all of Yourself – Your life, Your peace, Your righteousness?" And the answer came to his spirit, "Yes, that is exactly what I am saying." And Jones responded rather unceremoniously, "Wow, what a deal. I'll take it!"[10]

What we must be sure not to miss is this. Jones could not have come to this point without understanding something of how far Christ had gone to save him. He knew he had a load of stuff he could have never have gotten rid of without the forgiveness of Jesus. But he also knew that there needed to be a full exchange. A complete bearing of sin in the heart of the God-Man is the only foundation for true and completing forgiveness. Anything less is a diminishment of the gospel of forgiving grace.[11]

The fundamental problem with reducing forgiveness to legal pronouncements, market vocabulary or other forms of misappropriating the true power of forgiveness, is that they don't meet the demand of personhood. To be a person is to be in a relationship with another person. The 'image' of God in the created Adam and Eve is not merely an attribute. It is central to the meaning of being a created person. Imaging God included the ability to relate to the Creation in dynamic and intelligent ways. But it climaxes in the sharing of love between a husband and a wife followed by their enjoying the Sabbath rest of God. Sin destroys every level of that personal intimacy. The image is lost when human desire wins out over other-oriented love.

After Genesis 3 that prideful right to ourselves, self-idolatry, distances us from all trusting relationships. And that self-vaunting over any other is all we have ever known – until the arrival of the Lamb of God, Who is the Second Person of the Holy Trinity in the flesh. In order to reformulate or reconstitute the 'dis-imaging' chaos of sin He *had* to take on our flesh, and in that exchange He took into Himself all the de-personalizing qualities of my self-centeredness. That bearing, that carrying, that identification, and ultimate substitution at the very point of my own condemnation is the power of the overflowing love of the Triune God through the Son to all who would believe. Forgiveness has to be understood as making us persons again. The power of forgiveness in the whole schema of salvation is that it 'personalizes' everything that sin has done to shred the image of God in us.

A little girl expressed the profound simplicity of this theology of forgiveness when she asked a man who was dear to her where he had been. He told her he had joined others at a retreat trying to find out how to solve their spiritual problems. Her response was brutally honest. "Why didn't you come to me? I know the answer. Bring everything to Jesus."[12] He has welcomed all of us into All that He is. Forgiveness is the result of that powerful, personal exchange.

[1] A full treatment of all the words that produce the tapestry of redemption cannot be explored here. *Awon is found in Ex 32:32; apoluo*, to let loose from, release, Lk 6:37; and the Septuagint uses "to be merciful" (*hileos einai*), "to propitiate" (*hilaskethai*), and *apievai* "to cancel". See the brief but solid discussion in R.B. Girdlestone's *Synonyms of the Old Testament* (Grand Rapids: Eerdmans, 1978), 135-138.

[2] See the poignant explanation of the heart of Jesus in this regard in H.R. Mackintosh, *The Christian Experience of Forgiveness* (New York: Harper and Bros., 1927), 101.

[3] Col 3:3-4

[4] Charles William *He Came Down From Heaven* (Grand Rapids: Eerdmans, 1984), 51-52. As I write I have noticed an unusual amount of monographs that have come out recently on Is 53. It is a never exhausted prophetic resource for understanding the nature of the Holy One and the sacrifice fulfilled by Jesus Christ. Very few that I have found deal with the 'bearing' aspect of the Messiah in a theologically satisfying manner.

[5] It is crucial to emphasize the freedom inherent in this personal self-giving. Neil B. MacDonald's Barthian leanings are strong, yet helpful, in asserting that self-determination is at the basis of creation and redemptive relationship with Yahweh's people. Like Yehezkel Kaufmann *The Religion of Israel* and John Oswalt *The Bible Among the Myths*, MacDonald strives to keep God distinct from creation except for that which He freely determines Himself to do. The same freedom is to be found in all Christology. MacDonald argues that God's justice is always counter-balanced with His "desisting, forbearing" mercy from the Fall, through the Exodus and the Deuteronomistic history which lays the groundwork for understanding the work of the Messiah. See *Metaphysics and the God of Israel* (Grand Rapids: Baker Academic, 2006), 140-141ff.

[6] Charles Williams, *The Descent of the Dove* (London: Collins, 1963).

[7] Cf. Col. 2:9-10

[8] Girdlestone, ibid., 137 gives the same sort of outline.

[9] George MacDonald, in *God's Words to God's Children*, (New York: Funk and Wagnalls, 1888), 72-73, was the first to make it clear to me that neighbor comes from the one who is near to me, my "nigh-bor'. He writes convictingly of the call to forgive and thus to love one's enemy because all of us err, all wander and the realization that we are all liable to God's righteous judgment undoes all self-righteousness and opens the victim's perspective of the perpetrator in an equalizing manner. We will come to this issue more specifically.

[10] E. Stanley Jones, *A Song of Ascents* (Nashville: Abingdon, 1979). 52-53.

[11] I affirm the distinction made by Steve DeNeff in *More than Forgiveness* (Indianapolis, IN: Wesleyan Publishing, 2002), chapter 8 between 'policy' (legalism in any form) and love. See summary on p.164.

[12] E. Stanley Jones, *A Song of Ascents*, 235.

The story of Jesus that follows is misnamed "the parable of the unjust servant." As you read the passage below ask yourself who truly is the main character of the parable.

> "For this reason the kingdom of Heaven may be compared to a certain king who wished to settle accounts with his slaves. And when he had begun to settle them, there was brought to him one who owed him ten thousand talents. But since he did not have the means to repay, his lord commanded him to be sold, along with his wife and children and all that he had, and repayment to be made. The slave, therefore, falling down, prostrated himself before him, saying, "Have patience with me, and I will repay you every-thing." And the lord of that slave felt compassion and released him and forgave him the debt. But that slave went out and found one of his fellow slaves who owed him 100 denarii, and he seized him and began to choke him, saying, "Pay back what you owe!" So his fellow slave fell down and began to entreat him, saying, "Have patience with me and I will repay you." He was unwilling, however, but went and threw him in prison until he should pay back all of that was owed."
>
> **Matthew 18:23-30**

3

You Cannot Give What You Have Not Received

Said General Oglethorpe to John Wesley, "I never forgive."
"Then I hope, sir," said Wesley, "you never sin."

CONFRONTING A SHADOWY EXISTENCE

Frequently Jesus' most powerfully-stated points are followed with even more poignant stories. It is a rabbinic technique used by the master Teacher to clarify and to put truth deep in our spirit as reality, not just esoteric verbiage. Parables are a dynamic means of instruction and illumination. They cannot be simply distilled down to one concept. What is often revealed to me in my interpretation of these revelations from the heart of God, is how self-centered I am. Many times I can miss the main thrust of what Jesus is trying to communicate. To focus on the man who can neither receive forgiveness nor give it is to miss the central figure in the whole parable, the king. Forgiveness has its source in the heart of the master. The possibility of a life transformed by forgiveness in one who was in his service is a secondary matter.

We can be truly forgiving people. But how? Jesus used a method that turned theology into story so that we could grasp something of the grandeur of what He was revealing.

C.S. Lewis, in his fascinating book titled *The Great Divorce*, describes the real, substantive and solid people of Heaven talking to the shadowy people who are always merely looking at Heaven. The shadow-like have no substance, no worth and no value in themselves. Only that which is heavenly has value.

The angel, or the heavenly being, looks at one of these less than real men and beckons him to take the first painful step out of nothingness into reality and says, *Reality is harsh to the feet of shadows, but will you come?*[1] The continual challenge is to endure the pain in order to come to reality. Will you move out of the shadow kind of life and move into the reality of things? The imagined discussion continues with some revealing questions that uncover our inability to receive grace.

- Well, if I come there, will I be more useful?

- When I come there, will I have more talent?

- If I come to Heaven, will I be more productive?

Aware of this functional view of worth that in the face of grace is absolutely worthless, the heavenly being looks at him and says, almost laughing. *No, I can promise you none of these things. No sphere of usefulness: you are not needed there at all. No scope for your talents: only forgiveness for having perverted them.* Lewis is clear. We are offered only forgiveness. The angel confronts the idol of our own rationalism when he says to the shadow-person who never comprehends the essence of real grace offered freely, *No more questions, only answers, and you will see the face of God.*[2]

And the intriguing thing is that in the end this unreal individual in Lewis' story does not want to go into the reality prepared for him. He chooses not to go to a place of forgiveness. He only wants to go to a self-fabricated place where he can make things right or do things right in his own power, by his own perception.

Moving Into Deeper and Real Territory

I wonder if that is not what is at the base of what Jesus is doing in this passage. To clarify, Jesus is saying, "If you don't comprehend what you need from me, you will never know what the Cross is about. The result of your life will be simply trying to forgive up to the self-righteous number seven - or maybe up to 490 (if you are really "spiritual")." But Jesus says, *I'm talking about a forgiveness that's much deeper than that.*

The depth is grounded in the fact that true forgiveness is not a mechanical activity, nor a politically expedient working arrangement, and it surely is not simply being more useful to Jesus. Many of us live with what I call "emotional *détentes*" – where in our family, in our marriage, at our business and in our church, there are a series of humanly-contrived peace agreements. But those agreements are tenuous. They are not lasting because they are not sincere.

Most often, if there is a modicum of spirituality, there will still be the ever-present numbers game where the true idea of mutual forbearing and bearing is laughable. Of course, it would never be respectable to scream or throw a fit. But there is not a real covenant, a mutual familial commitment, at work at the foundation level in most of our relationships. There is simply a political arrangement. And it can be the worst torture in the entire world because both parties know that neither is really forgiven by the other person. Our little black books are cleverly hidden. The *détente* is a painful charade. It is purely functional. The parties are acting out because they have to or because it is the "Christian" thing to do. But all involved are damaged by falsity.

We are so functional with our stabs at forgiveness it must break the heart of God. Jesus' response and illustration are saying, *Peter, I'm not going to give you a measurable rule of what it is to forgive. There is no calculated rule in any relationship. I'm not going to help you solve the problem every time. I want you to dwell in the mystery of forgiveness. I want you to dwell in the Life of the Forgiver and out of that, you'll be able to work out these situations, maybe not easily, but they'll work themselves out because it will be Me that's working. It will be Heaven that's working this forgiveness out.*

Now, what is meant by that? I believe Jesus is saying forgiveness that is numbered and accomplished like a mere "project of holiness" never produces relationship. This means that in the mind of Jesus:

- Forgiveness is never a calculation.

- Forgiveness must include exploring the possibility of renewing a damaged or destroyed relationship.

- Forgiveness is also the willingness to open oneself to the possibility of further rejection and further disappointment.

Calculation is the word that helps me the most by uncovering any shadows of unreal forgiveness in me. My wonderful wife can tell in a moment if I'm calculating forgiveness. I am sure my children know. They can tell if I've got the number thing, the functionality thing going on. But forgiveness in the body of Christ is never a cover up. It's never a numbers game and it's never a mechanical activity. I believe there are people who actually think that forgiveness is mainly utilitarian. It is something useful in making life work – my way. The Lord is lovingly but insistently pushing us beyond that hazy manipulation to a much deeper reality of grace.

The Freedom from "Justice"

I remember a remarkable reflection on the question of whether forgiveness could ever be unfair. The author responded from a theological rather than an emotional vantage point. A Roman Catholic theologian was quoted saying, "As long as you cling to 'justice' you will never be guiltless of injustice. As long as you are tangled in wrong and revenge, blow and counterblow, aggression and defense, you will be constantly drawn into fresh wrong…. He who takes it upon himself to avenge trampled justice, never restores justice…. In reality, insistence on justice is servitude. Only forgiveness frees us from the injustice of others."[3] At least forgiveness provides a way to put a halt to the juggernaut of "justice." The process of bearing the wrong means that we are not hemmed in by the fear that the other will ever get what they deserve. They will. But that is God's business not ours.

You will recall our working definition of forgiveness included a:

- o **Process:** that is a real on-going relational process that involves a
- o **Bearing:** we have to bear the wrong-doer in my heart which includes a
- o **Willingness:** that is:
  - a. The willingness to put to death our sense of justice served, or to abolish any moral barrier toward another. Seen from another vantage point, forgiveness is the grace-enabled effort to volitionally relinquish every taint of resentment in one's heart.
  - b. This willingness is also conjoined to a heart that is willing to re-establish the possibility of relationship.

Let's look at an additional concept. If forgiveness means that sort of transformation, then we are on the right road to understanding what Jesus came to offer. It is much bigger than most of us can even comprehend, but forgiveness is at least the effort to put to death any residual resentment, to deal with the remnants of self-defined justice.

Remember how the parable Jesus uses blows the top off our insistence on payback. A king came to settle accounts, and the sum of the debt that the person owed him was a massive amount of money. Hyperbole does not quite define what Jesus does here. I have known some exaggerators in my day but this takes the cake. In a day when the daily news throws out millions, billions, and trillions so often that broadcasters have to enunciate clearly which letter starts each word because that they all sort of merge in the mind of the hearer, this may not seem like a lot. Whatever brings a cold sweat to the heart of a person who is familiar with the weight of an un-repayable debt – that is the understanding Jesus wants to evoke.

Here a servant comes to his master and asks for patience to extend the terms of the debt and this king says, "No, I'll go one better, I'll give you grace. Not patience, not condescension, I'll give you grace. I will cancel the debt." A clean slate, a loan completely paid off, a ledger with nothing on the debit side. How much clearer could a creditor be? But the debtor doesn't hear the message. What he does next is to go and violently demand justice from somebody else. He hasn't comprehended or received forgiveness.

Not only did the Master begin the process of forgiveness by bearing the burden of the debt, but he was also willing to renew a relationship with the one who had abused the relationship irreparably. He was willing to restore the man (and his family) into a place of responsible intimacy. The debt, the loan no longer stood between the lord and the forgiven.

Forgiveness is the Comprehension of Divine Grace

If forgiveness is not a numbers game, and if forgiveness means someone has to bear our wrong, then a third major point must be that the on-going process of forgiveness is always based upon a comprehension of divine grace. True forgiveness incorporates a transformative personal transaction which must be apprehended. The miracle of true reconciliation comes out of a relationship where something is given and something is received. In order to know forgiveness, Jesus teaches, we must comprehend divine grace.

There is not a more incisive and realistic assessment of evil than forgiveness. It is not a soft ethic. It surely is not cheap grace. It may be one of the strongest forces in all existence. Forgiveness is the uncovering of the true meaning of sin. It is an understanding of sin as a wrong heart that results in an actual wrongdoing. And there is no way out of the source or its fruit apart from a gracious remission.

Sin Revealed

The key to a biblical concept of sin is that it is always relational. Sin is not a thing produced in isolation. From Eden on, sin arises out of a broken relationship. The only thing sin can do is break other relationships. In the parable we have been discussing the astronomical debt was only the external problem. Something much deeper had transpired between the debtor and his master. Trust at the heart level was eviscerated by the apparent dissolute dealings with the owner's goods by the steward. So sin is best defined as a state of wrong relation; a state of rebellion that produces wrong acts, defiant acts, wandering, a squandering of what has been given. To move away from reception of grace is to always turn to ourselves from fulfillment or meaning. That breech produces only death, for none has life in oneself. Pride is the ultimate "isolater" because it rejects trusting another.

Sin Dealt With

All of us know exactly what outward acts of sin look like, but sin always comes from the heart that is warped by sin. Now, when the Old and New Testaments approach how sin is dealt with, we find some interesting verbs. Forgiveness can easily take on a philosophical air if we don't continually go back to the biblical idea of what it actually entailed. Remember our previous discussion: if one forgave, in the Old Testament, one *sent away*. Or, one *covered over*. Another word is to *blot out* or to *wipe away* a transgression. From another important perspective sin was *carried away*. A person *refused to keep the burden* imposed upon oneself by the one who sinned against you. In a real sense, sin placed a burden upon the victim and someone had to deal with that burden. The burden must be carried away.

    I have to be very clear on sin if I am going to begin to realize the full glory of what it means to receive forgiveness. But, likewise, it is also incumbent upon me to allow the exchange to take place in me. As I receive I must also give. That is why the Forgiver always turns to me and says, "Now, in order for My gracious gift of forgiveness to have its full end, you must forgive just like Me." Nothing about forgiveness is ever impersonal or non-relational.

    If what follows seems repetitive, it is – on purpose. We are masters at missing the point most of the time when it comes to the ethic of forgiveness in Jesus' name. Just like the steward missed his pardon, we can "get our ticket punched" and move right back into the shadows of unreality far from the heart of our Master's grace. If we are not going to repeat the obtuseness of the steward in Matthew 18, we must be fully engaged with what has transpired when we are forgiven.

Sending Another's Sin Away

    In our English translations, we often have simply our word *forgive*, but I think these other verbs help us to know better what transpires when the Lord says, "Stop counting and move to My heart for the resources you need to be a forgiver." You and I have the choice of retaining the burden or taking it away. We can keep it and let the unreality of resentment deaden our soul. Or we can send it away, cover it over, blot it out, wipe it away, remove it, and refuse it."

I think the Lord does all the things mentioned above, and more, for us when He pardons us. That's what the Cross means, and all the sacrifices of Israel were a picture of how our sins were sent away, covered over, blotted out by what the Lord does on the Cross. But we also must ask ourselves, Am I willing to truly forgive in that sense, with that same quality? *Am I willing to send away, to cover, to carry, to wipe away what somebody else may have done to me?* We must admit it is easier to sing about sins rolling away when they are ours than it is to allow them to roll off the ledgers of our hearts.

I have often tried to imagine the feeling that the priest would have had when he sent the scapegoat into the wilderness bearing the iniquities, the transgressions, the sins of the people of God.[4] There is much discussion of the meaning of the term *Azazel* (Lev 16:8, 10, 26). It might mean an 'entire removal' of sin. It could be a reference to another, distinct from Yahweh, to whom all evil is sourced. What is certain is that the graphic, almost objective nature of sin is undeniable here. Sin takes on a "thingness" that must be clarified. While sin has no physical weight, no tangibility, it is more real than we can acknowledge on our own.

But equally unmistakable is the importance of grasping the sole removal of sin through another's bearing of it. Interestingly, the verb for 'bearing' in Leviticus 16:22 is *nasah*. Our atonement lies in the fact that Jesus bore our lostness. His flesh – body and soul, was inextricably involved in remitting our sin-stained existence. He entered into the wilderness we produced. Our heart of self-curvature was 'transferred' not just *on* to Him but *into* Him. Of all the striations of biblical truth regarding salvation one wonders about the inclusive depth John the Baptist intended when he declared, "Behold, the Lamb of God who *takes* away the sin of the world" (John 1:29).[5]

Graciousness

Earlier, we discussed that in the New Testament the words and
the pictures for our spiritual problem and solution are quite similar to the
Old Covenant. To illustrate the reality of our need and its provision two
major words for forgiveness arise from the early church's experience of
salvation. The word to *send away* is very close to the Old Testament. And
the term *let go, to release* was mentioned as well. But there is also the term,
to be gracious to.[6] Forgiveness is to be gracious towards someone who has
sinned against us. It is "to grace another" with what they most desire or
need, but they also know they do not deserve.

These words may carry many of the same basic connotations
in the Old and New Covenants, but the radical difference is that in the
New Testament we are forgiven through Jesus alone and called to offer
forgiveness in Jesus' own name.[7] There is no grace without Jesus Christ
at the center of its meaning. He lives out in the flesh all the promises of
release from the penalty of sin promised to Israel. He alone can forgive
sin as the Son of the Father in the self-giving power of the Spirit. The
doctrine and practice of forgiveness can never be removed from Jesus –
not ever.

We forgive just as Jesus has forgiven us. In the New Covenant
forgiveness is aligned with a whole new conception of reality. We move
from promise to Fulfillment, from system to Person, from shadows to
Reality.

All of us need someone who will bear our burden.

When I was growing up in Taiwan we were often surrounded
by villages of Taiwanese people. One day on our way to our school bus I
passed a crowd of neighbors just outside our front gate who were visibly
agitated. They were focused on the doorway of a house I passed every
day. When I asked what the fuss was all about I was told that the owners

of the house were trying to unseat the demon of that place. (Outside of the West the 'other' world is an ever present fear-producing reality.) I watched as four men, each holding the leg of a small chair, writhed in a ritual dance trying literally to overthrow the evil presence. They soon were spent, of course, and in apparent failure yielded to the Buddhist priest's next offering. A boy, not much older than I, stepped forward. His eyes were fixed in a sort of trance-like semi-consciousness. The priest removed the youth's T-shirt and then the boy began his own form of chaotic choreography. In a couple of moments the priest handed him a sword. As he continued to sway and lurch the young man began to lacerate his back with the sword which had razor sharp edges, like a saw, on one side. The blood began to pour and to sprinkle the ground around the youth. He did not stop until his blood had covered the threshold of the house.

It was nearly a decade later before I accepted the forgiving grace of Jesus, but in the meantime (and ever since) that experience marked me. Even in my most unreflective years it was clear to me that I, that all of us need a Mediator. There is no freedom from the evil in our hearts without Someone to pay our debt. Every religion has its own shadow of that reality which points to Jesus only. All of us have written into our consciences the need for Another to take our place. I have watched atheists become agnostics in a moment of panic. I have heard agnostics rant against God for the problem of evil. I have witnessed pew-sitting moralists cry out to Jesus when their lives begin to unravel. We are made for a Mediator. We have no answers to the stark pain of life without Another bearing our anxiety. All of us need the blood of Jesus to remove our sin.

There comes a time when we realize that forgiveness is not a numbers game any longer, or a *détente*, or an insincere calculation. We can come out of the shadows and walk in, sometimes harsh, but gloriously freeing reality. For reality is defined by a Person: Jesus, and the way by which:

>He bears away,
>
>He carries,
>
>He sends away,
>
>He covers and,
>
>He wipes away all sin.

Forgiveness, for Him, is a free act of grace and if we are to forgive, we must also comprehend that grace in our own lives. In the name and through the Life of Jesus I now can forgive those who have wronged me terribly.

The Meaning of For-Giveness

I don't often find good theology in the *Wall Street Journal* or the *New York Times Magazine*, but occasionally there are articles that confirm biblical teaching.

Many of you may know the name of the late William Safire, a marvelous essayist. I'll never forget the morning that I opened up the New York Times Magazine and found his discussion of one of the many words that is misspelled in our culture. He was quite exercised about the confusion.[8]

One of the misspellings that really bothered him was the word, "foreword", which he often found abused in the foreword of books. Since then, I've never ceased looking at that first page of a book to find if it is a foreword or a forward. He was right. It is shocking how often the word there is misapplied. He went into this irritated discussion in terms of explaining the etymology of the prefixes. He said if you use the word "for" with the letter "e" after it, as a prefix ("fore"), what you

mean is that there is something that is prior, something that comes
in front of. If you write a *foreword*, it's the word that comes before, so
the word must bear the prefix 'fore'; not 'for.' *Forward* can mean to go
ahead, to move forward, but a *foreword* is a word which comes ahead
of other words. Then he said if you use the prefix "for" it means to
prohibit, to refuse, to neglect or to fail. So if I forbear, it means I refrain
from bearing.[9] If I forbid, it means I no longer bid. If I forget, it means
I refuse or neglect to get, and if I forgive, it means I refuse to give to
somebody what they deserve to be given. Therefore, the abuser is not
given their due.

I looked up from that essay and experienced a sort of
theological epiphany. I know I am slow on the uptake but I thought,
"Had I heard the word "forgiveness" ten thousand times and never
really understood its meaning?" I was embarrassed by the numerous
unmindful times I had talked and preached and prayed about
forgiveness, but it had never dawned on me that forgiveness is a
refusal; a refusal to give to someone what is rightly theirs. For-giveness
is to simply say, *I am not going to give what that person really deserves.*

Then I began to understand something more about what Jesus
does in His forgiveness of me. He for-gives. He understands it, He
properly judges it, but He refuses to give me the problem back. He
chooses not to give me what is due. Here the glorious exchange takes
place. He takes what I am through what I have done - upon Himself.
He brings it into his own heart and flesh, and He removes it and covers
it, imbibes it, absorbs it on my behalf. As Isaiah put it, "Surely he took
up our infirmities and carried our sorrows" (53:4 NIV). I lose my sin
because He refuses to give me what I deserve and in exchange He offers
His grace-life. What He gets is what I give - my sin. And He does not
give me what that sin entails. That which is my due, He takes. What is
my debt, He assumes and He *for-gives* me. When He refused to give me

what I deserved I was for-given. God forbid that we should ever forget that only He is able to forgive.

I now look at forgiveness in a whole new light. When I know I've wronged my Lord, I realize that His heart for me first is not wrath alone. Forgiveness *involves* the heart of the Eternal Holy God with my sin. He takes all of me and my action into His own holy heart. He takes what I deserve. He incorporates His own righteous judgment. While all that was necessary for salvation was, as the Reformers used to say, "made over to me" in the atonement, my appropriation of that work is as real and personal as any restoration of relationship. His heart for me is a desire to remove the moral barrier to relationship with Him that I instigated. His gracious release involves not giving to me the brokenness that I've incurred. Instead He gives what I must receive in order to be reconciled. He's willing to enter into relationship again with me, and by His grace He gives me the power to respond in kind.

A beautiful summation of this point is found in a discussion on justification by faith where our reception is defined as "the apprehension of God's love in Christ."[10] When I realize and appropriate the fact that He is the Source of my life; that I am drawing all of my life from a measureless reservoir of grace, then forgiveness begins to have its full effect.

If Received it Must be Given

What is received must be given. I must not repeat the mistake of the steward when hecompletely missed that unbelievable dispensation of unmerited grace. God gives me the power by His authority to restore a broken relationship. However, that result is not guaranteed. The other person involved may remain in willful rejection of restoration, or even non-volitional insensitivity; what is crucial first is my heart. I am only ultimately responsible for what is in my own skin, as one of my confidants once taught me. And note: what is not received cannot be given. That explains the ludicrous actions of the man in the parable who never even knew that the king had forgiven him; that his lord had erased his overwhelming debt.

Could it be that we miss the parable's true point when we read it? Let's just take verse 27. Broken into its component parts we have:

The *lord* of the slave

Whose heart has turned in *compassion* to the undeserving

He *released* him of all that he owed[11]

He *forgave* him all of the *loan*[12]

As we study the topic of forgiveness, how do we approach this verse theologically? To be honest, most of us are primarily focused on the 'debt' which is our problem. The reality lies in all that preceded my debt. The debt is quite real, but not nearly as real as what precedes it.

I think we misname the whole scenario, which shows us how focused we are on ourselves. The parable is not about a wicked servant or an unjust servant. The parable is primarily about a king. I have never seen a translation that has sub-titles that reflect the true theology of the parable.

If you observe the original language it literally flows like this: *Having had compassion, the master of the slave, loosed him the loan and sent off him.*

It is not debatable; the major player is the king not the schemer, the defaulter. The point of the gospels is to look at Jesus. We are called to focus our attention on the One who has in His name the authority to forgive and chooses to forgive because He is so graciously holy. The Gospel is based upon the history of Israel's relationship with the Triune God whose mercy (*hesed*) is always at the forefront of His love for His people. Compassion is His nature.

So the focus is first of all a kingdom in which the king is in charge and not those who mess up the account books by our conniving. He is eternally holy and that is seen in his compassionate, righteous and gracious self-dispensing abolishment of what justly should be given to us. Forgiveness always starts in the heart of a person. The Person who forgives in this parable reflects the heart of God.

I began to ponder the range of metaphors which indicate divine forgiveness in the Scriptures. The pictorial presentation has been there all the way through, but Jesus shows us in this picture an expression of what this forgiveness looks like. Remember Isaiah 38:17, where Hezekiah's supplication includes the radical belief that when God forgives, all sins are *thrown behind His back*. Is that a double negative? Behind the back would be…the front! But it is simply an expression that tries to contain the mystery of forgiveness. He carries our sins no more. Jeremiah 31:34 states, *"He remembers your iniquities no longer."* And in Micah 7:19, *"He throws our sins into the depths of the sea."* Most of us know these verses.[13] We use them all the time in Christian worship. The first response that arises out of a comprehension of this grace is gratitude in awe and praise. That may be one reason why most of the creeds use 'forgiveness' as the fundamental term for our relationship with God. If we start there worship ensues.

Some sayings are so well-worn in evangelicalism that we tend to shy away from using them. But in all my life I have not heard a more comprehensively astute and helpful assessment of forgiveness than that spoken by the modern saint, Corrie ten Boom. She said that *When we are forgiven, Jesus throws our sins into the sea of His forgetfulness.* You see, she'd read Isaiah and Micah. He casts all of our sins into the sea of His forgetfulness and He puts a sign there with two words - "No fishing". She knew biblical forgiveness. Most of us must admit we don't. We are neither willing to receive nor dispense it. We choose the shadows, not the real.

The Difficulty of Receiving

Why is this so difficult? I remember hearing a long time ago that the two most often misspelled words in the English language are "receive" and "believe." I think that is more indicative of a theological problem than a language difficulty. Let's face it. It is one thing to acknowledge that our sole source of hope is a supernatural one, but it is just plain hard to accept. Forgiveness is hard to receive, and as a result it is hard to give. Charles Williams poignantly indicates that, "It is not easy to be forgiven; certainly not to continue in the knowledge of being forgiven. Only the princeliest souls can bear it naturally for long."[14] Forgiveness includes an instantaneous release but it is the foundation of all on-going relationships.[15]

Many of us live our lives within the church, Christian marriages and families much as the steward in the parable did because we have missed the King and the "justice" He refuses to give. He does not respond like the king we construct. His heart is both righteous and merciful. His authority is holy love. We've missed a comprehension of divine grace and, therefore, all we see is an extension on the debt. We have this remarkable amount of talents given to us - the amount given here is well into the millions of dollars in present economic parity. There is no possible way for this debt to be repaid at all, ever. Yet this man comes and says, "Please have patience with me." He asks exactly one time and is extended forgiveness. But then he quickly adds the clear indicator of missing grace at its source when he says, "I'll pay it back." A lack of receptivity of grace carries a grave reality check. We are well-skilled in refusing to be totally dependent. We want to help grace out. Surely it cannot be that I have to live in a reality I don't control at all! And it is right here that we soon meet our limitations – usually a lot sooner than seven forgivings. If grace does not source our life our debts will never end.

Why Would Jesus Exaggerate So?

Jesus said it was a debt of *ten thousand talents*. It may be that I am dwelling on this because we have just sent our third daughter to a Christian university. Private education in America brings with it a monthly bill. There are days when the exaggeration of Jesus in this parable does not seem far-fetched when I look at the contents of that envelope which indicates what I owe.

I did a little digging when I began looking at this parable extensively and found that the entire taxation of first century Palestine to the Roman government was only a *hundred* talents. Herod the Great was a megalomaniac; money, buildings and self-exaltation comprised what he lived for. In his yearly self-payment, the most he ever gave himself was nine hundred talents. (The steward owed 1000 talents.) In our day when amounts of exorbitant debt have produced numbness in us, we slip too quickly away from the abject impossibility of repayment intended here. How many times a day do we hear that some company can help us out of our mountains of debt in every direction – for a fraction of the amount due?

So we have an extreme statement by Jesus to make His point: this billion dollar debt could never be repaid. Like sin, this debt was not going away. Once incurred, it was there forever. Whenever the master even crossed this steward's mind there was that millstone of hopelessness. The debt was just too much for this man, or anyone, to ever handle. Yet because this individual could not comprehend anything of divine grace, any grace at all, he couldn't receive the grace offered.

It is very similar to a portion of the parable of the prodigal son in Luke 15 which we often miss. The prodigal son comes back home. Many brilliant minds have analyzed the prodigal's speech that he carefully memorized while still in a faraway country. I know he uses the word 'sinned,' but he does not truly comprehend grace. He is not receiving. He is calculating, negotiating terms, even commanding his father. He's not asking for true forgiveness. In his processed speech he tells the father, *"Make me like one of your hired servants"* (Luke 15:19). Why? Because he intends to pay back what he took. The Father cuts him short as the monologue takes shape a second time (Luke 15:21-22). He interrupts the negotiation, which grace always does, and lovingly corrects by an overflow of external expressions of an internal deluge of grace already bestowed.

Why is it we insist on not receiving what is given? The Lord's response to our consistent missing of the point is, *No, I don't want a servant; I want a son. Not a 90 days same as cash debt reduction plan, but a clean slate. I am not interested in a worker, I want a familial relationship.*

We still think that somehow when we come to Jesus with our stultifying debts and He clears the deck, that He doesn't really mean it. He's not really fully forgiving us. There has to be a hook in there somewhere. We're going to try to pay Him back this incredible debt we owe Him. The servant is looking at amazing grace from the most powerful person in his life and all he can say is, "Please extend the terms. Excuse me for not paying you back yet. Give me more time and I'll get it paid back." He is looking at an excuse for his debt and is constitutionally unable to comprehend grace, compassion and radical forgiveness. Paying back provides control. Receiving requires humility.

In verse 27 it says the king "had compassion." The word is *pity* and gets pretty graphic in the original. It's actually *an internal tenderness in the bowels* - the bowels of mercy we often read in the King James Version. That's very close to what's going on here. The insides of this king are turned in compassion toward his servant and the servant can't comprehend it. This king is not giving patience. This ruler is not giving an allowance for an extension of the debt. This lord is giving internally motivated mercy. This master is offering tangible grace. The only currency of this monarch is the currency of stark, unmistakable grace for those willing to receive rather than to sign a repayment plan.

I believe there are many Christians who have never fully comprehended that palpable mercy. We preach it, we pray it, we try to proclaim it, but we have never truly received it. The grace of our King says, *You don't owe me back because I love you from within my own being and because this is my Kingdom, run My way. I refuse to give you what is due to you. You must be free. I will carry you and take away every barrier. It is up to you to do only one thing – come and receive what I offer.*

It's amazing to me what happens next. This king releases him, the one who owes him the billion dollar debt. We forget that realistically what the debt required at first would result in the death of the family. There was no hope for a swindler or his family if this kind of deception was brought to justice. The man was not only freed from economic justice, but from death. He was freed to honorable relationship.

Imagine the freedom of a family whose provider and parent is released by the king. The entire family is released to be free. No one has to be shackled, imprisoned or reminded of their humiliating debt. In fact, Jesus is so precise here that we have a change in language. The king cancels not the *debt*, he cancels what he now refers to as the *loan*. He makes it a different transaction. Yes, the master chooses to carry the debt, but the servant could have looked at it as something that he had produced out of his own wrong use of economy. The king changes even the nature of it. There is not only economic freedom but psychological emancipation as well.

Forgiveness is based in the personal reality of the Trinity. Our Judge and King is not simply after a reduction of debt or the removal of punishment. He is offering a relationship of intimate love and trust. Unless we understand that, the entire universe becomes a huge numbers game. Jesus offers only friendship. There is no other way to truly know Him in the Spirit to the glory of the Father. How easy it is to miss the wonder of forgiveness.[16]

The king says first I will *free you from the loan*. Second, *I cancel it entirely*. And third, *I restore you to your prior office*. He is not only forgiven but he is imbued with a trust that was lost. This last point is implied, but similar to the gifts of the prodigal Father, there is every indication that the abuser is placed back in a position of responsible stewardship. He says nothing about payback in kind. There is no contract now that necessitates kindness to others. He says, *No, I forgive you the loan; and by the way, you can come on back and work here again.*

Sadly, this steward did not get it. And, devastatingly, neither do many of us.

If I could use a word picture here; we need to stop and recognize that there is a funnel of grace pouring through the top of our heads; ceaselessly flowing from the heart of the Triune God. It is a grace that is Life Itself. This grace covers debts and restores hearts to their proper receptivity. If we don't receive that grace, we will never be able to dispense it. If, as many have stated, pride is the foundation of all sin, then it may be that we have a parable here of one being too proud to be forgiven. That may be the crux of the matter for all of us. Until our mechanistic, justice-based, self-centered pride is put to death we never enter into eternal life. If Life does not enter into us then we cannot offer it in humility to another who is as undeserving as we.

This forgiving grace is pouring down. He offers release. He cancels the debt, the loan. He restores us to our former office. If we don't receive that, I believe the results in our life are stress, bitterness, resentment and wall building. If we receive His grace, we can turn bitterness to hope, and lack of love to gracious offering of His life. If we receive, we can give.

Chrysostom (c. 347?–407 AD) preached on this parable with a consistent refrain pertaining to the gentle, forming grace of God. He viewed the debt as rejecting all the gifts of God. But grace is found in the heart of the lord. Our view of kings and judges is inadequate. The One who gives Himself, according to this early biblical interpreter, 'reckons accounts' with "unspeakable tenderness."[17] Like a good father, the king was lovingly challenging the apparent crime; teaching as he confronted the debtor. Chrysostom reads a plea even in the last strong encounter with the unjust servant. He benevolently reminds the hard-hearted man of the grace offered but which was revoked not by the king first, but by the very act of unforgiveness which followed.18 When seen from this perspective it is unimaginable that anyone would misunderstand the offer. Simply unimaginable.

[1] C. S. Lewis *The Great Divorce* (New York: Macmillan, 1978), 42.

[2] Ibid., 43.

[3] Philip Yancey wrote, eight years after his first article on forgiveness (that I have mentioned (see note 1) as being so influential in evangelical circles), this penetrating reflection on a modern holocaust after WWII, the ethnic cleansing in Bosnia. He refers to Wiesenthal and the dying guard here as well, 'Holocaust and Ethnic Cleansing: Can Forgiveness Overcome the Horror?' *Christianity Today*, August 16, 1993, 27.

[4] Lev. 16:20-22

[5] The exact title, "Lamb of God" is used only by John here, it is found nowhere else in Scripture this exact way. There is no place in the OT cultus where a lamb is specifically determined to 'bear' (nasah) the sins of Israel. See *Theological Wordbook of the Old Testament* (Chicago: Moody Press, 1980) vol. II:658-659 for a good summation of the options with the term Azazel which is hard to determine from it sole usage in Lev 16.

[6] *Charizomai* in Greek, used for a canceled debt (Lk 7:42-43), release of Barabbas (Acts 3:14), but also of forgiveness in 2 Cor 2:10, Eph 4:32, Col 2:13;3:13.

[7] Acts 2:38, 5:31, 13:38; 22:16; Col 1:14, 3:13; Eph 1:7, 4:32

[8] William Safire *New York Times Magazine, Nov. 7, 1986.* Just yesterday in a scholarly book I found the author using the word "forego" when he actually meant to use "forgo", to not do something. Safire's concern, I have found, is well merited.

[9] Interestingly, 'forward' is the English contraction of 'fore-ward' so that the rule expounded here still applies even if a vowel is lost by usage. English is messy. There are always exceptions to the rule laid down here for emphasis. See "for- and fore" in *A Dictionary of English Usage* ed. by H.W. Fowler (Oxford: Oxford University Press, 1965), 205.

[10] H.R. Macintosh, *The Christian Experience of Forgiveness* (New York, Harper and Brothers, 1927), 125.

[11] The term for release is from the Gk. apoluo used 19 times in Matthew. This is the only time it pertains to forgiveness or a release from a debt of any kind. The only time there is a similar spirit in the use of the word is when Joseph pondered 'putting away' Mary when he found out she was pregnant (1:19)

[12] Notice that the term for 'debtor' (v.24) is now changed to a 'loan' (v. 27)

[13] Cf. Isa 44:22 "I have blotted out your transgressions like a cloud and your sins like mist; return to me, for I have redeemed you." Oswald Chambers reminds us here, "When God forgives, He never casts up at us the mean, miserable things we have done." "I have blotted out, as a thick cloud, thy transgressions, and, as a cloud, thy sins." "A cloud cannot be seen when it is gone." *The Place of Help.*

[14] Charles Williams, *Forgiveness of Sins*, 84.

[15] I think this is what has exercised Greg Jones so much in his *Embodying Forgiveness*. The relative isolating of the sinner from the full ministry of the Body of Christ at any point produces a doctrine of forgiveness which devolves into what he calls the "therapeutic" conception of pardon. The less-liturgical and ecclesiological might not be convinced of his argument but in the span of Church thought his concerns are well placed.

[16] Macintosh, *Forgiveness*, 24,30,33, 60. In his irenic way Macintosh takes on the liberal theological giant, Ritschl. He questions whether liberal theology has any notion of the true nature of sin and forgiveness. In that loss of wonder by diminishing what only God in Christ has done is the loss of salvation.

[17] Chrysostom, *Homilies*, Homily 61, NPNF 10:378.

[18] Ibid., 10:378-379

> *And the lord of that slave felt compassion and released him and forgave him the loan.*
>
> **Matthew 18:27**

4

For Us and For Our Salvation

> I believe in the Holy Spirit,
> the holy catholic Church,
> the communion of saints,
> *the forgiveness of sins,*
> the resurrection of the body,
> and the life everlasting.
> Amen.
>
> *Portion of the Apostle's Creed*

FORGIVENESS IN THE FLESH

I graduated from seminary in 1983. It was a wonderful time of engagement with the Word in the fellowship of like-minded disciples of Jesus. Out of all the exams, sermons, exegesis papers and projects I produced, the assignment that left the most profound impression was a paper for which the professor assigned the title:

The Relation of the Incarnation to the Atonement. At first flush, that might seem like the most basic and rehearsed concept in Christianity. But he knew, and I soon found out, that reflection on that subject is really not common at all.

As a teacher for nearly a quarter of a century I have kept that assignment a tradition in my theology classes. Each year my students moan just like I did about the lack of good sources on the topic, the hours of hard reflection, the difficulty in distilling the key points that issue out of such massive theological ideas. A couple of years ago I told that teacher, who had become one of my best friends, that I did to others as he had done to me. He smiled and confessed that one of his professors had required the exact same topic in his seminary training.[1] Misery loves company. Let me add, that in all of my years of teaching nothing, to my knowledge, has been more transformative in my student's lives than that reflective assignment.

Revelation always precedes theological reflection. Though a tome should be written on the relation of the person of Jesus Christ and the Atonement, it would behoove us to stop at this point in the trajectory of the meaning of forgiveness charted thus far. It is imperative to recognize that no doctrine or ideology, no matter how truly orthodox, that can ever replace the nature of the One who spoke the words of this parable. His words are the universe from which theology lovingly strives to chart a course. Maps can only point to reality. I am often shocked by how quickly my interpretation of the parables really is an immediate opportunity to think about myself. Forgiveness, for the Christian, must issue first from the self-revelation of God the Son.

While scholarly interpretation debates how the parables of Jesus as a literary genre relate to rabbinical modes of teaching, it is often the case that Jesus places the key figure right at the beginning of the parables. I have often wondered why we skip the recurrent emphasis on the father of the prodigal son and go right to the sinner. Could it be that we impose our interpretation of Luke 15 too quickly on the text and miss Jesus' main point?

In the parable of Matthew 18 it is easy to identify with the unjust servant, for we are he. But, it may be that our primary focus, or first reflection, ought to be on the king, the lord of the servant. All of us are involved in the drama of the parable due to our immediate identification with a desperate debt, but that need is not met by a legal or judgmental dictum. It is dealt with through a Person. The Word alone is never sufficient for the Christian. We are committed to the Word made Flesh. That is what is Real, True and Holy. There is no forgiveness apart from Him. Grace always precedes sin and thus both transcends it and delineates its cure.

Forgiveness in the Context of Matthew 18

We have outlined Matthew 18 and now we must see the relation of this parable to the rest of the chapter. A gracious king offers remission of a debt without requirement to a slave who misses the grandeur of offered grace. That lack of receptivity has two results. The servant remains both un-forgiven and unforgiving. Thus, rather than being forgiven and freed he would be soon be judged and condemned. It is also wise to look at where in the gospel of Matthew this chapter appears. In the larger scope of the book Matthew's gospel this chapter comes near the pivot point in the book. There is a shift from daily ministry to the actual passion of Christ.

Some have said that the gospels are passion narratives with really long introductions. Matthew has taken eighteen chapters to prove to us that the King of Israel has come in the flesh.

At the beginning of chapter 19 there is both a geographical and dispositional shift in Jesus.[2] This departure from Galilee would be his last. In this actual, historical, geographical region prophesied about and now fulfilled in the earthly ministry of Christ this parable is placed as the final words which Christ offers before his departure for Jerusalem. Matthew records this discussion concerning forgiveness. By chapter 21 Jesus has made His entry into Jerusalem on the back of a donkey. Forgiveness is never merely a statement, a legal dictum, a dispensation of judicial fiat. It cost the life of the One who spoke the parable in order to speak of the reality of forgiveness.

Jesus had lauded the disciples for recognizing the revelation that He was the Son of God in Caesarea Philippi (Mt 16:13-20). But with that recognition there was an accompanying revelation of a different mindset than that of the Messiah of God. What has been true even though He was acknowledged as the "Christ" becomes unmistakably clear; Jesus meets an assortment of hard hearts: Pharisees (19:1-12), self-centered disciples (19:13-15), a young ruler whose heart is ruled by what is not good (19:16-26), followed by a parable which illuminates the pride in those who think their commitment somehow trumps grace (20:1-16). It is on the way to the Cross that Jesus has to rebuke his disciples. Once, that correction includes the mother of two of them. Her sons were so focused on gaining power and position that they totally dismissed the purposes of their Messiah. They attempted to alter the scandal of the Cross prophesied by Jesus (20:17-28). The story of the physically blind being healed is miraculous support for the deity of the Son of Man but also occurs at the climax of the disciples' spiritual blindness in order to highlight how far from the mind of Christ they are (20:29-33).

Forgiveness from the Heart of Compassion

In contrast to these hearts curved in on themselves is the other-orientation of the King.[3] It is very interesting that the last verb used to describe the ministry of Jesus prior to Jerusalem's agony is 'had compassion" (Mt 20:34) which is identical to the pivotal verb in the parable on forgiveness (18:27).[4]

As noted earlier this term, compassion, is about as intense a description of love turned outside toward another as can be found. Think of the love of a mother for her child, especially when in distress, and you will begin to see the vibrancy of the term. It is the term Jesus uses (Lk 15:20) when the father sees his prodigal son coming home. Compassion is literally, to "share passion with, or for, another." It is to passionately focus one's full being towards the need of another. When the inner love of another takes on this internal bearing it is truly a pathos that alters both the bearer and the one borne.

My dad was a gentle man. I remember him correcting drivers who shared the road with him in Taiwan. "Be careful," he would shout in his perfect Mandarin but nonetheless in vain in the midst of the chaos which went by the name "traffic". That is about as loud as I ever heard him express impatience. One night, however, I heard a very different tone of voice, when I crossed the line in disrespect to my mother. I remember the mixture of pain and anger as he rose from the stair on which he was seated. He came uncomfortably close to me and said, "Don't ever talk to my wife like that again."

His anger brought me to my senses immediately. I retreated to my room in distress. The rush of emotion soon dissipated and I was left to look at myself. Shame and remorse cascaded over my

soul. I had known Jesus for awhile but He had much yet to do with
my inner life. I couldn't sleep due to the pain I had brought into
our home. In the dark of the early morning I heard the door to my
room open. I knew what I deserved. I saw the figure of my bath-
robed father heading determinedly toward me. As he approached
I quickly rose from my bed. I braced myself for what was to come.
I was taken aback when he embraced me with quiet but resolute
strength. He had already showered and shaved. I don't think I ever
loved the scent of Old Spice before that day but I have loved it ever
since. I trembled with remorse. But through the darkness and in
the warm enveloping arms of my dad I sensed the heart of divine
compassion. He affirmed again his primary love for my mother but
then he said, "Son, I love you too much to let you damage yourself
by that kind of attitude. Let's work through this together." He bore
me in that moment of compassionate forgiveness. It was as if a
shaft of cement was laid at the foundation of my heart. He gave me,
by grace, a sure substructure upon which to change and to grow. I
was secure, loved, built up, and offered another level of maturity. I
never talked with disrespect to my mother again.

One must remember that compassion, like grace, is not just
emotion. It is not some divine "stuff" or a spiritual nod of the head.
Compassion is personal and costly. It is an expression of the Life of
God when holiness meets the needs which sin produces. God is so
moved by our need that He does everything necessary to take all
that our disorder produced into Himself. Compassion, to be truly
effective, in redemption must be shown through one who actually
knew our despair. God may have been able to fix things from a
distance. But He could not transform us in a personal way at a
distance. Compassion meant taking on our human condition. There
is no saving compassion without the Incarnation.

The Gospels and Forgiveness

The actual number of references to "forgiveness" (aphiemi) is not overwhelming when it appears in the ministry of Jesus. It is possible to actually find "sections" in His life that are similar which seem to bring a focus on forgiveness in the synoptic writers:

- John the Baptist preached for repentance and the forgiveness which the Jews believed would come when the Messiah would set up His Kingdom.

- The man let down through the roof by his friends provides an interesting statement about the Son of Man and forgiveness early in his self-revelation.

- Jesus was witheringly strong on the warped worldview that produced blasphemy against the Holy Spirit and was therefore unforgivable.

- Peter's discussion with Jesus about the number of times one is to forgive occurs in Luke as well as Matthew.

- Jesus offers forgiveness to a sinful woman with language very similar to the paralytic.

- The comment about the cup in the Upper Room was tied to his blood that would be poured out for the forgiveness of sins.

- And there is that unbelievable statement of Incarnate Holy Love from the Cross, "Father, forgive them for they know not what they do."[5]

Noting the conspicuously few references to forgiveness in direct relation to the person of Jesus in his earthly ministry, the brilliant, Swiss, Catholic theologian, Hans Urs von Balthasar (d. 1988) has suggested that a fuller doctrine of the relation of Jesus to divine forgiveness might be seen if one started with the epistles and worked backward to the gospels.[6] His argument is a strong response to those who attempt to diminish the atoning work of the Savior in His actual self-perception and ministry. All of the reality of forgiveness is present in the historical Jesus. The epistles are the Spirit-inspired reflections on the reality of who Jesus was and what He revealed.

Balthasar notes, unlike John the Baptist that Jesus offered "unconditional" forgiveness in contrast to the potential legalism that over-emphasizing repentance might afford. Rather than outlining steps to forgiveness Jesus "claims" people for the forgiveness that flows from the Triune God. We are left with the joyful task of piecing together the order of salvation. Repentance and faith are crucial but it is not the first thing Jesus says in the context of forgiveness. He speaks and it is so. There is something we must grasp theologically before we apply it to our own brokenness.

But most helpful is Balthasar's discernment of the personal participation of the Son in the humanity of all He loved and served[7]. The Incarnation was a study of and an engagement with our real condition. Jesus of Nazareth learned the effects of sin on true humanity. It was not an accident that the revelation of forgiveness was first connected to the physical touching of sin-broken bodies. When Jesus touched He assumed. He took into Himself that which could not be dealt with apart from His real life and loving heart.

Most miracles have at base the mutual self-surrender of physical need met by the actual body of the Deliverer. Every miracle and teaching then becomes a leading of people to the deeper need of forgiveness. Jesus took on the burden of the needs of those around Him. By His "absorption" of the destructive consequences of sin into Himself He would expunge them all upon the Cross. He offered more than a religious upgrade. Jesus actually came to share our life as one who was not a stranger to sinners. His identification with us was deeper than any of the preceding prophets. When He asked His disciples about what the common person thought of Him the first response was, "You are a lot like Elijah, Jeremiah, or other prophets who bore Israel in their souls."[8] There is only One who chose to take our burden into His own being, to identify with us at the most fundamental level, to share all that was necessary in solidarity with us in order to bring about a total redemption (Heb 2:14-18). Only what Jesus bore is ultimately healed.

This bearing by the Savior is affirmed in multiple ways. In a summation of the early Galilean healing ministry of Jesus, Matthew quotes Isaiah's prophecy regarding the Messiah as one who "took up our infirmities, and carried our diseases" (Mt. 8:17). Peter looks back at what he missed while living in proximity to the Lamb and writes, "He himself bore our sins in his body on the tree." But as he draws the implications of holiness of heart and life that result from a full appropriation of that 'bearing,' he ends the same verse with yet another allusion to Isaiah 53 writing, "By His wounds you have been healed" (I Pet. 2:24).[9]

H.R. Macintosh underscored this perception of the acute, palpable reality of forgiveness as he responded to the question of Jesus being able to forgive before the Cross actually occurred. Recognizing the mystery involved there and reflecting on the Incarnation of the Son he wrote:

As for His (Jesus') mind, as everywhere in Scripture, the Kingdom is built upon the forgiveness of sins. Such a work cannot be done mechanically or from the outside, but only through experience. It can only be done from within the sinner's situation, its misery and sense of condemnation. There is a sympathy which does not stand aloof, content with words, but which descends into the depth of need, and lays hold upon another's burden. If we picture Jesus face to face with one of the penitents who encountered Him…we may ask ourselves precisely what it was in Him that conveyed to them the sense and reality of pardon. What created their assurance? Manifestly not the simple fact that He admitted them to His presence, or that He looked at them, as a spectator of their misery. Rather it was that in spirit He went down to where they were, in their bitter, grief-stricken distance from God; and that thus joining Himself to them inwardly He took hold of their hand, that He might raise them up.[10]

Forgiveness is Trinitarian

What is intriguing is that nowhere does Jesus say, "I forgive you." He may say, "Your sins are forgiven." But He does not pronounce forgiveness in the way we would expect. There is no doubt that He has the authority to forgive sins, but He refers to the Father forgiving and that sins will be forgiven. While a full orbed doctrine of salvation must incorporate all references to one's reception of the work of Christ, it often seems we separate the person of Christ from the activity of the Savior. It may be that the incorporation of the passive tense, are forgiven, is meant to include an understanding of forgiveness that is profoundly Trinitarian. This is worth exploring. Just as it is devastating to separate the Person of Jesus from His work it is also injurious to unwisely limit salvation to one Person of the Trinity.

Jesus is undeniably clear about His purpose, which was to reveal the Father (Jn 14:9,10; 17:1-5, passim). He came to show us the Father through the indwelling Holy Spirit. His dependence upon the other two Persons of the Trinity breathes in every page of the Gospels. Each of the miracles of Jesus was a distillation of the Triune power over creation and humanity particularly. The words of Jesus are the understandable communications of the incomprehensible language of the Trinity. Forgiveness is the work of God contracted in a way that is receivable by us who have no idea with Whom we deal in reality. The King has every right to 'settle accounts' in abject, unyielding exactitude with each of us, but He has chosen to forgive out of a heart of compassion.[11]

We don't often think about the conversation within the Triune Godhead when it comes to us. For good reason, we should tread softly and humbly in the face of such grandeur and mystery. But, George MacDonald imagines what the Father might have said as He sent the Son to forgive all of us in the name of the Triune God:

> Let them see what I am like; go and be Myself amongst them. You can do it, because You are my son; they are My sons, but they cannot understand the Father until they get some idea of what the real Son of my heart is. Go to them, and dwell with them, and suffer them, and let them do anything to you they like, so that they may see what I am… they won't believe Me; go and be amongst them as My very Self.[12]

Forgiving is not merely an act of sending or not giving what is deserved, it involves the whole Life of the Triune God. This is most clearly revealed in the Incarnate Son and His Life poured out "for us and for our salvation," as several of the major creeds of the Church state. It would be wrong to seclude references to forgiveness from the One who offered that precious gift to all He ever met. His very Being bore all the vicissitudes of sin. Jesus' power, whether to forgive or save or recreate, was, and is, always derived from the Father in the Spirit.

The heart of the Triune God is most clearly revealed in the actual life of the Son of God. Holy compassion is never more sacred or transcendent or real than when it is revealed by the Messiah. Each time he utters forgiveness of sins all three Persons are revealed in the Lordship of the Godhead. His heart is the heart of the Father and the Spirit perfectly expressed because Jesus never thought of forgiving alone.

It is also very interesting that Jesus reserved some of his harshest words of the impossibility of forgiveness when it came to the difficult concept of 'blaspheming the Holy Spirit' (Mt 12:31, Mk 3:29). So present in every person's life and salvation is the Spirit of God that Jesus makes it unmistakable that if one attributes evil to the goodness of the Spirit's actions there can be no forgiveness. Forgiveness is a co-equal endeavor for the Triune God.

Forgiveness is Only Offered in the Flesh

Jesus forgives but never stops to expound through a theological syllogism the transfer of guilt, the bringing of our sin into His actual life. He fights the satanic temptation, from the beginning of His ministry until Gethsemane, to offer forgiveness in any other way than through His own Body. The passivity of the verbs, "you are forgiven", "poured out for the forgiveness of sins", always entailed the entire full-bodied activity of the Person of the Son. His forgiveness was never by word alone, it was only offered through the Word who took our flesh.

Where Jesus is forgiveness is literally offered. It permeates the gospels. Even a superficial recounting of His ministry proves that He came to release us from what we deserve:

the forgiveness prophesied in the midst of the Jordan,

the remission of sin which flowed to a man who could not move physically,

the pardon that confronts all that stymies worship and clouds relationships;

the word of release pronounced over the life of a woman full of sin.

All of these accounts come from the Only Life that can forgive because He is forgiveness. Every step in the land was that of the pure, holy, Incarnate God who knew every sin of every one He encountered. He gave His Life away so that sin could be taken in and taken away – through His earthly, human, physical, body.

Jesus looks at several people which the gospels record and says, "Your sins are forgiven." In fact, what He is saying is, "I am the only One who can truly forgive." It is in the union of transcendent self-revelation as Jesus of Nazareth that any forgiveness for humanity's sin has ever occurred.

Whenever we remove forgiveness from actual daily life it becomes an immediate idea that we think we can manipulate. That is why so many of us are walking wounded. We have never really let the sin done against us go to the only place it can to be forgiven – into the very body of Christ. There is no cavern large enough in the universe in which to cast my sin. And even if there were, nothing would happen to the sin itself. It would remain. But when Jesus is allowed to enter into any situation of wrong-doing there is unrestrained hope.

The Incarnation was the fullest expression of personhood in all its glory. Jesus' self-giving love meant that He loved us more than He loved Himself. He assumed our humanity in His body. That humanity perfectly united to His divinity as the eternal Son provided the perfect union of our problem (volitionally absorbed by the One True Man) and His provision (Col 2:9-10). The Atonement is not a function, it is a Person. Forgiveness is offered when the Son, in the flesh, offers Himself. Our being forgiven is from within the full divinity and humanity of Christ.

Paul alluded to this mystery when he wrote in II Cor. 5:21 *For our sake he made him to be sin who knew no sin, so that in him we might become the righteousness of God*. If sin, from one vantage point, can be viewed as the dissolution of our being – a turn from what is real to that which is unreal, damaging and worthless, then the only way for sin to be dealt with is to be destroyed at the very place where it first began its work – in a human being. And the only actual, historical place where that can happen is in the Incarnate Christ, the Son of God who became the Son of Mary.

None of us know what kept the sinless One from becoming sinful but sin came as close to His eternal, pure glory as was necessary in order to pardon us and to offer us a new creation through His Body. The exchange He inaugurated in Himself is not a shadow play. It is the ugly, dirty job of the Only Savior of the world. The reality of what He has done for us is sufficient to meet the abject loathsomeness of sin with resplendent, reconstructive redemption.

For this reason, the historicity of the creation of Adam and Eve, the Fall, the Incarnation of Jesus and His death, resurrection and ascension to the right hand of the Father is absolutely crucial. Other religions may speak of forgiveness but it is rarely a relational understanding and it is never actual or total.[13]

It is only here, of all of the history of religious figures, that One would dare to offer forgiveness without an immediate focus on the particular actions of the sinner who is being released. He offers "unconditional" forgiveness as Balthasar contrasts Jesus and John the Baptist. John gave a list of ethical commands to those who sought to be baptized. The Lord does not offer a list of 'do's" or "don'ts" except where He says, "do not sin again" (Jn 8:11). The undeniable implication is that only the gracious heart of God could do such a bold thing. The Pharisees, in all their pride and obtuseness, are close to reality when they questioned Jesus' absolution by asking, "Who can forgive sins but God alone?" They are unwittingly nearer reality than many today who are carrying the burdens that Jesus alone has borne on their behalf in His own body.

The Stark Reality That is Forgiveness

The point of this theological excursion has been to ground everything we are saying about forgiveness in the nature of God as incomparably revealed in Jesus Christ. No normal person ever looks at sins done against them in an other-worldly way. Wrongs hurt. Sin causes pain. Whoever wronged Peter was surely not enabled to forget they had done it. Peter would be sure that the person never did. That's the problem with religious numbers and personal relationship – there are libraries of resentment in that schema. So how is the difficult ministry of forgiveness to transpire? It must be offered through an actual beating heart; the heart of the Son of the Father by the power of the Spirit. And anyone who wants to be in that lineage will have no other kind of forgiveness to offer.

True forgiveness is as real and as unmistakable as the offense. In essence, it is more real than the wrong. For true Christ-like forgiveness is more aware of the relationship than of the hurt. The person who is forgiven has experienced compassion that transcends the wrong done. All forgiveness that comes out of a life set free contains the same Life that resides within the heart of the a wronged person. Spirit-empowered forgiveness forms the perspective before, during and after a wrong.

If you have ever truly been the recipient of the kind of compassion expressed here you know how abjectly gritty forgiveness is. At the intersection of all sin and redemption forgiveness resides as a beacon of hope against utter despair.

I used to have a negative reaction to what I considered the 'mystics' who kept talking about seeing Christ in the poor, in one's neighbor, in the sinner. But I am beginning to grasp the reality and gravity of their true read on reality. Augustine wrote:

> *Remember that in Christ you have everything. Do you want to love God? You have him in Christ. Do you want to love your neighbor? You have him in Christ, for 'the Word was made flesh.'*[14]

We have a diminished view of the Incarnation. Jesus became an actual human being when He "took on" flesh. As a man He identified with all that we are. We have discussed some of this as we looked at the baptism in the Jordan. Immanuel, God-with-us, has come and He has interlaced our life with His. So that when we serve another we are ultimately serving Jesus. That is not a demeaning of the other. It is their created purpose. When we forgive we are making Jesus the center of the person who has committed the trespass and we are claiming that Jesus is the One who makes that transaction possible. To forgive is to relinquish all power into the nail-scarred, compassionate hands of Jesus.

Forgiveness seems like the most unjust action in the world until Jesus is brought into its dynamics. He is able to release, redeem and reconcile all parties involved. He judges every motive, every actual wrong done flawlessly. He offers Life and hope and restoration relentlessly. It is our part to allow Him to take center stage in our tragedies. Anyone who has truly experienced forgiveness, either giving or receiving it, knows that it is a transformative reality. It bears the potential of becoming a 'soul-transporting' reality where we are lifted out of abject self-centeredness into the other orientation that is the foundation of being made in the Image of God.

---

[1] I have, since beginning this book, found that the generations of teachers involved in this question may go back even farther than I have thought. See the introduction to H.R. Mackintosh *The Person of Christ* (Edinburgh: T&T Clark, 2000) ed. and introduced by T.F. Torrance.

[2] Space disallows us the privilege of a book length survey. Let the following outline suffice:

	Narratives	Discourses
1-4	Messiah	5-7 Foundational Truths for Disciples
8-9	Ministry	10 Training Disciples for Mission
11-12	Preaching	13 Kingdom "in" Disciples
14-17	Discipling	18 Discipleship in the Kingdom
19-23	Last Ministry	24 The Coming of the Kingdom
25-28	The King's Passion, Resurrection, and Commission	

Charles Talbert notices in the special training of the disciples that intensifies as the Passion draws nearer that 17:24-27 deals with the difficulty of relating to the "outsiders" (temple tax and Peter's questions) which is followed by the entirety of an "insider" discussion (relationship between 'brothers') 18:1-35. C. Talbert, *Matthew*, 216-217. He also has a very helpful note on the textual variants on 18:15; "If your brother should sin' (variant adds 'against you'), changes the actual contextual emphasis somewhat while not altering the overall theology of forgiveness. Ibid., 219.

[3] It is interesting to note that there is a word that is not translated from the Greek in the text. Literally it reads, "Through this was the likened the kingdom of the heavens to man king." Scholars say this is a repetitive term, a pleonasm, which it may be, cf. Mt 22:2. In what follows however there is also the possibility that the real nature of a person underscored by *anthropos* is a part of the power of this engaging parable.

[4] Actually Matthew uses this term *splangdizomai* five times in all. If one takes this usage in the parable as pointing to Jesus the term only applies to Christ in its usage in this gospel.

[5] Any review of a concordance on the words forgive or forgiveness will give the interested student support for this view of the 'arenas' of forgiveness in Jesus' life and work. It might be also illuminating to see that they seem to fall more toward the very beginning and then the very end of His earthly ministry. What also catches our attention is the relative scarcity of usages in the rest of the NT as well.

[6] Hans Urs von Balthasar, "Jesus and Forgiveness," *Communio* 11:4 (1984), 322-334.

[7] Ibid., 331.

[8] Mt 16:14; Mk 8:28;Lk 9:19

[9] The Greek words for bear in these passages are *airo* and *lambano* which are both resonant of *nasah* in Hebrew as we have seen above. Eph 1:7 is similar in import, "In Him we have redemption through His blood, the forgiveness of sins..." Cf. Col 1:14, 20, 22. Col 2:13 takes a unique tack in this same vein. Jesus cancels *(exalepsas aorist active participle)* the debt, or bond which stood against us with its legal demands and 'took up' *(airken present indicative active)'from the middle'* an idiom which when combined with the verb connotes putting something out of sight. Whatever the translation it points to what Jesus assumed on our behalf. See *The New Linguistic and Exegetical Key to the New Testament* ed. Rogers and Rogers (Grand Rapids: Zondervan, 1998), 464-465.

[10] Macintosh, *Forgiveness*, 215-216.

---

[11] Cf. George MacDonald *God's Words to His Children*, 37. Most of us would not know George MacDonald without the stamp of approval given him by C.S. Lewis. It is common to find themes that MacDonald explored percolate out of Lewis' ruminations.

[12] George MacDonald, *Getting to Know Jesus* (New Canaan, CT; Keats Publishing, 1980), 49.

[13] It is argued that in the ancient Greek philosophers one cannot find a clear reference to forgiveness. Aristotle hasone related reference but the translation has to be forced to come near to what the Christian meaning of the word entails. *Nicomachean Ethics* trans. W. D. Ross, Bk.6:11, "This is shown by the fact that we say the equitable man is above all others a man of sympathetic judgement, and identify equity with sympathetic judgement about certain facts. And sympathetic judgement is judgement which discriminates what is equitable and does so correctly; and correct judgement is that which judges what is true." Other translations force "sympathetic judgment" to mean "forgiveness" without much support.

[14] Maura Sée, *Daily Readings with St. Augustine* (Springfield, IL :Templegate), 28.

Remember that the servant has come to his master and has been forgiven, or at least externally released. His debt was remitted because the master felt and expressed compassion. That compassion is more real than the debt owed. It is the solid rock of unchanging grace that is rejected by the man who could not receive it. Rejecting reality always produces relational carnage. He left the king's gracious presence and immediately returned to a legal definition of debt and forgiveness. His relentless transaction of debt and payment produced a conniving harshness that resulted in his own guiltiness which would not be forgiven.

Now at Mt. 18:28 the story changes radically and for interesting reasons.

But that slave went out and found one of his fellow slaves who owed him one hundred denarii; and he seized him and began to choke him, saying, "Pay back what you owe." So his fellow slave fell down and began to entreat him saying "Have patience with me and I will repay you." He was unwilling however, but went and threw him in prison until he should pay back what was owed. So when his fellow slaves saw what had happened, they were deeply grieved and came and reported to their lord all that had happened. Then, summoning him, his lord said to him, "You wicked slave, I forgave you all that debt because you entreated me. Should you not also have mercy on your fellow slave even as I had mercy on you and his lord."

Matthew 18:28-33

5

Forgiveness Costs Everything

Remember that we said forgiveness:
*is the process in which a wrongdoer
is borne in the heart of the wronged,
and is not given what is deserved,
and the wronged is willing to allow the possibility of
a reestablished relationship.*

Note this is always a relational process, not simply one you do a
certain amount of times to assent to some cultural ideal of civility only
to be followed by granting ourselves a free ticket for retribution if we
run out of patience. It is a process that occurs in the heart as a receptor
of grace, in the mind as a volitional choice, and in the attitude of one
who's been deeply wronged. And this process will cost heavily. In fact,
it may take death to your own sense of justice and your very self if
forgiving grace is to flow from your heart.

Forgiveness can never be a function which denies relationship.
True forgiveness is aware of the numerous barriers that we can erect

for all sorts of righteous reasons. In contrast to these many obstacles it always encourages relationship. This is not to say that forgiveness means that you'll never have a difficulty again with a friend or loved one. It also does not mean that we have to submit to an abusive situation without intervention or protection. Nor does it mean that a person will be transformed overnight by your forgiveness. That is the stuff of hour-long TV programs and unrealistic movies. What it does mean is that the heart of the wronged is so transformed by the renewing grace of forgiveness received that a door of hope is found for the damage done by sin, offering the possibility to be redeemed and restored. No relationship is ever easy if it is an honest one. Forgiveness resists isolation. It is the arch-enemy of self-pity and narrowness of spirit.

Over the years, I have had several opportunities to interact with people who have heard me preach or teach on forgiveness. It is interesting to me that out of all I preach it is the one topic that elicits the strongest responses and reactions. Most often, those rejoinders are reservations revolving around the extent to which forgiveness should be given.

At this point it may be good to take an honest assessment of the real issues we face day by day. Let's apply a bit of what has been covered above to some of the things that we actually face. How does forgiveness apply to:

A mother or father who kills their baby out of anger?
An abortionist or those that comprise that culture of death
A man who rapes and murders a young woman?
A man who sexually abuses children?
A minister who has repeatedly taken advantage of women?
A person who corrupts a weaker person and is unrepentant?
A person who consistently slanders while claiming to follow Jesus?

I certainly am not claiming that forgiveness is easy – ever. It is, quite possibly, the hardest reality in the universe. It cost God everything. Am I willing to hear His call upon my life regardless of the cost to me? Can He define the edges where His judgment, His absolution start and where the place of forgiveness must be found in my heart?

I appreciate the honesty of those who say, "You have no idea how hurtful the relationship I am in is," or, "Are you saying that I am supposed to submit to that kind of abuse again?" I have tried to distinguish between the seriousness of sin in its actual expressions and the counteracting divine bestowment of forgiveness in the midst of the carnage. Forgiveness never overlooks sin or treats grievous transgression with mere sentimentality. In fact, forgiving another may be the most exacting discernment of the defiant self-centeredness of which all sin is at base. To forgive another is first a radical form of self-knowledge. That is exactly where the servant in the parable failed. The reality of forgiving grace was not allowed to show him who he really was. Thus, true forgiveness reveals pride in both the perpetrator of sin and that which is possible in the one sinned against.

No rational person argues that Jesus would desire an abused person to remain in the middle of a relationship of destruction. Though we are all unable to read the mind of God in many situations, we know that He came in the flesh to set us all free. But, there are many situations in which the cost of forgiving must be paid where there does not seem to be an immediate rectification of the wrong. Judgment ultimately belongs to the Lord. That often harsh reality must be faced as we yield ourselves to the ministry of forgiveness defined by the Cross.

Since our focus so often turns to our sense of right, it might be wise to first check our own uncanny ability to hide ourselves from

the expense of true forgiveness. We are responsible for what goes on in our own skin no matter what the offense toward us has been. A biblical theology of forgiveness is neither theological pabulum, nor is it a trendy accoutrement for a humanistic culture that has no real doctrine of sin. The church has had its fill of pop psychology.
This is costly stuff.

DEFENSES AGAINST FORGIVENESS

A forgiving relationship – and more particularly, a restored relationship – always takes a miracle of grace; grace that we must open ourselves up to. With most human hearts that grace has to push through substantial barriers. Robert McGee uncovers several defense mechanisms which are typical for most people who are either unforgiven or unforgiving. Interestingly, each of these can be seen in some way in the parable in Matthew 18.

- The first one is *chaos*. A preacher once defined most of my life with a phrase that has stuck with me for decades. He said in order to be healed we have to be willing to enter into a 'tunnel of chaos' first. When a serious wrong occurs, chaos ensues. And that produces an incredible amount of strain and stress. So we construct an excuse based upon the carnage. We say, "I'm so stressed, I can't really respond to this person because it just is so difficult for me. It's just too hard to comprehend. I don't want to have to deal with all of this turmoil."

- The panic that chaos tends to produce can lead to a history of unresolved devastation. There are people who are enchained in their *past pain*. Largely due to the lack of confrontation needed to move out of chaos, we stack up little black books of unresolved relational issues.We soon are inundated with histories of brokenness. They simply say, "I'm not going to risk loving anybody anymore. It hurts too much."

• A third barrier results from our lack of dealing with stacks of wrongs we have lived through and that is, *re-injury*. There is a critical mass that is produced if we don't forgive; we keep injuring ourselves and other people by our silence, by our bitter spirit, by our lack of openness. We actually do more damage to ourselves than the original offender if we stay behind this barrier.

• I have found Magee's findings confirmed in myriad ways on the fourth barrier. It is the seemingly impregnable fortress of *bitterness*. Most people know who have suffered from internal resentment it is not something that dissipates easily. In fact, without divine intervention it stays, grows, and influences all other areas of life. The immediate emotional pain may subside, but the least little similar action can cause an explosion of rage.

• The saddest thing is when the barriers in our own hearts become the excuse for *continual conflict*. A couple can be always engaged in conflict because one or both parties have never truly forgiven a hurtful parent or an abuse at church. You can have homes full of a miasma of conflict because no one has received grace. We end up building walls even in Christian homes - against peace, against physical health, against relationships, against emotional growth.[1]

Might there be enough grace received, enough of the presence of the Lamb of God, and the resolve to dispense what we have received to pray along different lines? It will feel like it is costing us everything to pray something like this:

> *Lord, you did not keep a pile of my debt for me to look at all the time. You dealt with it. You did away with it. It's gone. My billion-dollar spiritual debt has been wiped away. I have been sinned against but that is not the end. With you it is never the end. Now, Lord, take this resentment, take this weight of debt for which I am responsible. I have kept it within my own heart. Change my inner being that I may never become a calloused grievance debt collector.*[2]

That is a tough prayer. It is a costly prayer. It is, for most of us, the only kind of prayer that breaks the bondage of the barrier of bitter revenge.

De-Personalizing as a Barrier

Jesus drops a hint of the depth to which we go to hold on to wrongs that can be easily missed by the modern mind. In the appalling reaction of the totally forgiven servant to his unsuspecting colleague, we are told that the graced man has the other sent to prison (Mt 18:30). In Roman law only a certain amount of debt could be the basis of imprisonment. Thus, the first gentleman, who had the debt that had been forgiven and couldn't forgive his friend, had to actually lie about what had been done to him. In that period of human history, one could not imprison another person for an amount owed that was less than their actual value (or, "a hundred denarii"). In Roman law, the amount that was owed was far less than that which one would pay for a slave.

That portrays a graphic first century picture that we replay often in less overt but nonetheless painful ways. The unforgiven becomes the unforgiver. He goes to the torturers (18:34) and totally misrepresents what had occurred. Out of hard-hearted resentment and the ludicrous notion that he is still able to repay what was impossible to restore he seeks to take his companions freedom away.

I am convinced most unforgiveness is based upon our own perverted view of reality. Sin causes every form of stupidity. And if we have a numbers-orientation to wrongs done, accounts kept and resentment stored, what has been done to us may easily become our total preoccupation. Chesterton famously stated that insanity was not doing wrong things but doing the same thing over and over again. That is true with the victimization mentality that our barriers to forgiveness can produce.

Let's be clear here. There is not one whit of diminishment here of the horror of sin done to anyone. Sin is destructive to all it touches. But grace is more real and it is thoroughly reconstructive where it is allowed to flow. And grace never inflates debts. It confronts real problems with real people on both sides of the sin, both giver and receiver. We make up things that are distortions far greater than the actual offense, so we do not set people free because we allow resentment to accrue with the wrong done. The mix can be destructive all around. We must guard against exaggeration that can be a form of lying to ourselves, lying about the perpetrator, and probably lying to God.

At the risk of being too personal, let me tell you where the Holy Spirit convicts me more than anywhere else – in the shower. I don't know what that ambiance does to make me more malleable but it is often there where my exaggeration of the 'wrongs' that have been rehearsed in my mind are shown for what they really are – lies. In a moment of sane reflection I have to admit it has never been a "million" times that that affront has happened. The perpetrators do not "always" do what my hard heart has kept sealed and carefully numbered. I have had many 'conversations" with wrongdoers behind that curtain where I have extracted a pound of their flesh in indignant anger.

Jesus never would have us look away from sin or treat it lightly. He never did. But he also did not lie about, exaggerate or dwell upon offenses. He had a different perspective. It was rigorously honest. Who else would dare look at a man paralyzed for life and tell him he needed his sins forgiven without mention of his physical malady. Forgiveness always tells the truth about everyone involved.

Like this man, our hardened hearts produce a battery of barriers that say to those who have transgressed against us that they are quite literally worthless to us. The forgiven but non-receptive debtor in the story says to the one who owed him a paltry sum in comparison to his own, "You are less than a person to me." The result of that is an uneasy détente founded in a deeper, de-personalizing power play. The best a relationship can get at that point is the relational equivalent of a tense and tenuous arms reduction plan. We need what compassionate forgiveness provides: a different perspective on people that only a continual comprehension of grace affords.

We talk a lot in politics about different countries and fears about wars and accumulating larger amounts of warheads. Treaties are frequently defined by agreements to reduce what has been accumulated. The exact same politics can exist in our relationships. We become emotional machines with hearts encased in a rigid calcification of bitterness. Unable to work toward any covenantal resolution, we settle instead for the often vicious battleground of waging an armament reduction. Not being really fully forgiven, or forgiving, we simply reduce the arsenal. But the threat of those siloed missiles is always there and everyone involved knows it. We live with a constant spirit of mistrust and emotional tension.

I remember one of my counselors years ago said to me that it's unnerving to find a tick on a dog. Ticks are, basically, blood-sucking parasites leeching off of a living host. But the really sad thing, he said, is that in most human relationships we often are two ticks and no dog. Two ticks, two people sucking the life out of each other because they cannot forgive and there's no living host in between. My wife says that people who can't forgive are like the living dead. There is simply no life. There are walking around but inside they carry this heavy debt within.

BREAKING DOWN THE BARRIERS TO FORGIVENESS

Re-Personalizing Grace

To forgive we must pay a huge price. It will cost us everything. It means that we will look at sin for what is really is. We must face, not excuse, what was done that destroyed fellowship. And we must refuse to depersonalize the one who treated us with such inhumane disdain. That is a key. We who have tasted grace must refuse to lie about any aspect of the deed or the doer. We must be willing to re-personalize the perpetrator of grievousness. That means we have to be willing to be restored: to break out of the chains that have threatened to bind us. We cannot wait for grace to change the antagonist. *It must start in us.* However, it can never be accompanied by the self-conscious claim to spiritual superiority.

George McDonald writes that when God speaks to a person and says, I forgive you everything, He is at the same time calling us to, *Come out of sin will you? Come out. I am the light, come to me and you*

*shall see things as I see them and hate the evil thing. I will make you love
the thing which now you call good and love not. I forgive all the past.* That
is exactly what happened when the king forgave the servant. But
barriers to forgiveness abounded still.

If we could just understand that one sentence – *I forgive all
the past*, all of life would be different. Listen to what McDonald says
in writing about our all-too-frequent response. He continues with
the pretended conversation. Often we, as ungrateful recipients say
in both our words and actions, *I thank you, Lord, for forgiving me, but I
prefer staying in the darkness.* And then we add quite presumptuously,
Forgive me for that, too. McDonald, interpreting from myriad Scripture
passages the voice of the Lord, writes, *No, I cannot forgive you that
too. The one thing that cannot be forgiven is the sin of choosing to be evil,
the sin of refusing deliverance. It is impossible to forgive that sin. If I did, it
would be to take part in your sin, and I can't do that. If I did that, it would
be to side with wrong against right, with murder against life. I cannot
forgive that. The thing that has passed, I have forgiven, but he who goes on
doing the same, annihilates my forgiveness, making it of no effect.*[3]

MacDonald is spinning out the deadly serious implications
of rejecting that which is proffered. I am sure the easy thing for us to
say about this sort of recalcitrance is, "Lord, I know somebody like
that." But I must first look at my own heart for what is really there.
I must be yielded and vulnerable enough to pray, "Holy Spirit, am
I willing to bring my heart out into Your light? Is there any element
in my spirit where I have been a willing participant in that kind of
attitude?" I perceive that the Lord says, in the strongest of terms,
*Don't choose to live as if the Spirit was the evil in your life and your evil is
your good. I cannot be there if you live there. You will never be forgiven if
you insist on retaining any hint of unforgiveness.*

Earlier we touched on the Trinitarian nature of forgiveness and mentioned the place of the Holy Spirit in that offer of grace. Without the Spirit there is no conviction of sin, no application of the work of Christ, and no internal assurance that we have been forgiven. To remove Him from the process is to deny forgiveness entirely. No wonder then that Jesus' strongest statements about unforgiveness pertain to how we deal with the Holy Spirit. [4] When we recognize the Third Person of the Trinity as the One who restores true personhood both in us and in the one who has sinned against us, then there can be talk of real forgiveness and willingness to enter back into the 'tunnel of chaos' in order that the relationship might be raised from the dead.

Forgiving Irregularities

In this re-personalizing process we will be called to look at others with the heart of compassion which removes barriers to forgiveness. One of the most surprisingly helpful books in my life is Joyce Landorf's *Irregular People*. It came across my path in an overwhelmingly difficult time relationally speaking. I was dealing with a couple of people who seemed to find joy in destroying safety and intimacy. Despite numerous attempts to clarify why they were causing consistent pain and strain, I not only failed to find a solution but I sensed they were not even willing to face the issues that were causing such ongoing grief.

As a result, I began to harbor in my heart both helpless resignation and soul-deadening resentment toward them. This book came to me as a source of amazing spiritual release of my own consternation. Landorf outlined three areas normally present in these irregular people. Her points perfectly described the difficult people

with whom I was dealing. I was a Christian. They claimed to be
Christians. Yet my relationships with them were spinning into chaos
at every point. There were insurmountable barriers everywhere. I
checked my heart. I examined my attitudes. I scrutinized everything
and found that nothing from my part really altered the ever-present
tension.

Landorf said, *irregular people* are always **emotionally blind**
and they will probably never change from being stunted in that way
until heaven. No matter how you try to communicate your pain, they
do not, and will not, see your need. They will not look into the issues
that serve to destroy mutual love. They simply are unable to see what
hurts you, so their words or their responses are always coming out of
emotional blindness. It is more than ridiculous to try to change them at
that point. Landorf's first element applied to my difficult relationships
immediately. They could not see anything about the unresolved chaos
that had become an acceptable status. Emotional detachment hinders
healthy relatedness.

The second thing she said about *irregular people* is they are
emotionally deaf. They cannot hear you. Talking, pleading, and
praying are ineffective. You may even be in a context where supposed
mutual openness is encouraged but that is never really experienced.
The church is full of this emotional handicap. The sharing of real pain
caused by another is seldom, if ever, present. The few brave enough
to go there are often met with this crushing deafness. In my own
experience of this handicap I inaccurately deduced that this lack of
response was somehow *my* responsibility; that I should be able to
inaugurate mutual communication with convincing clarity.
I hoped that I could somehow win them over to at least a civil
attentiveness. Surely the Holy Spirit would open up an avenue to
enable mutual listening. Again, noting that many people are

blind and deaf to relational disorder was freeing. It was reality producing for me to see that I did not have a spiritual wand that I could wave to bring change to these relationships. Their inability to hear the pain they were causing was not my fault.

Landorf's third point was that *irregular people* are always **unable to speak**. They are blind, deaf and they are verbally deficient, challenged in communication as well. Sure enough, the folks with whom I was yearning to be reconciled were unable to communicate even the most simple, loving statements. They were absolutely unable to affirm or to share their hearts. They could not talk the language of love.[5]

The book set me free. Prior to reading it, I thought that all people were like me, or at least they should act like me toward me: open (often to a fault), desirous for understanding, and willing to talk about most everything. No. Many people just aren't like that at all, and *irregular people* are definitely not like that. And they will not change before they reach Heaven. Only the Lord can judge whether an irregular person is in sin in their inability to respond. It may be a volitional hardness which makes relating even more difficult. What I began to learn is that I could forgive and move into life without the nagging feeling that I was not free. I did not have to live shackled by other's ineptitudes, their infirmities or their iniquities.

This reflection became personally challenging. I had to allow the Lord to move my heart to a whole new level of understanding and offering forgiveness. There is no guarantee that the recipient of grace will ever comprehend, much less acknowledge their need of forgiveness. A person who is emotionally handicapped can be the most difficult to relate to. If the one shut out is not careful, barriers to forgiveness can be set up within the heart that stand in mute defiance of the pardoning grace which must flow if Jesus is present in power.

When I realized the number of people in my life with the infirmity of a desensitized spirit, I was convicted of a deeper need in my heart. It seemed that the Holy Spirit was asking, *Bill, are you able to forgive somebody who will never see your pain? Who will never hear what's going on in your heart? Who will never be able to express what you'd love to hear them say to you?* Probably one of the deepest workings of the Spirit in my life was His enabling this kind of prayer: *Lord, I want to be made like that. I know there are going to be people like this in my life all of my days. I don't want to walk through life with a numbers game view of forgiveness, never comprehending your grace and never experiencing the cost of forgiving.* The removal of barriers in our heart when the offending party does not even recognize a speed bump is a work that necessitates the sanctifying power of the Holy Spirit. We are called to re-personalize at the heart level even when the barriers to full restoration are left unattended by the offender who does not recognize the relational destruction they leave in their wake.

Dealing with our Dungeons

I remember once hearing a joke which said a pessimist is one who builds dungeons in the air. Not castles, but dungeons. A schizophrenic is one who builds those dungeons and then moves into them. I think that's right. But I want to add to the schizophrenic the unforgiven person. This is the one who moves into those dungeons in their spirit often out of guilt. They may not be clinically schizophrenic, but the guilt of not being forgiven is just as traumatic as residing in a dungeon that is made from the flawed mortar of narcissistic perception. Like so many characters in famous novels that are offered freedom but return to the small, dark, airless security of their personal prisons. They have become comfortable with no freedom.

Many of us have never let our chains fall off when we are forgiven. All defense mechanisms need to be checked, cleansed and ordered by the Holy Spirit. We need to make sure that we don't build false, self-protecting fortresses and lock out peace. We need to resolute that we don't lock out any possibility of restoration that the Holy Spirit offers.

Hopefully, as you have followed the argument here, your heart and mind have come to ask the Forgiving Savior to shine the light of His exacting holy love throughout your heart. Maybe you are an *irregular person*. Maybe you are grinding away in a seemingly unrecoverable relationship. You may have given up. There is no use in trying to communicate. Barriers and dungeons abound and you have lost hope.

Regardless of the lack of emotional health in the one who needs our forgiveness, we still need to be cleansed within from all dungeon-like barriers to the free flow of the nature of God in us. I want to ask you some things before we end this chapter:

- Have you been able to face all of your own guilt?

- Have you been able to name the source of that guilt?

- Once you have been honest enough to name that origin of shame completely, all of it, not hedging one moment on the truth, can you acknowledge that it has robbed you of your life?

- Can you look the whole ugly thing and its consequences square in the face?

If you can, then I would like you to look at that other person who has hurt you and with ruthless honesty name that sin done against you. Do not think this is a billion dollar debt. It may only be a twenty-five dollar debt. Name what has transpired for what it really is. Don't make it bigger than it is. Be brutally honest with yourself. Don't repress it. Don't excuse it. Face the issue and name it for what it is. I am convinced that if we don't name it, we're not going to be able to fundamentally and finally deal with it. The largest barrier to be overcome is to put away any lack of truthfulness (Col 3:9). With this hard work done, there is more honesty to pursue. To break the barriers that de-personalize another, there are three levels of accountability:

- Acknowledge the sin to God.

- Acknowledge it to yourself as the Lord reveals what He is asking of you.

- Acknowledge it to some other human being.

I John 1:9 and James 5:16 are absolute truth. If we confess our sins honestly to Jesus and to one another, we can be healed.6 John Wesley said that one of the reasons that Catholics were so much healthier than evangelicals was because they had someone besides God to confess their sins to. One of life's most difficult challenges is to forgive someone who is oblivious to the deep pain they have caused us. But that difficulty is nothing compared to the sin of not confessing our resentment. Those who claim to walk with Jesus cannot abide with "acceptable" sins like resentment, bitterness, or hard-hearted rejection of those who may have wronged them. What seems like an unbearable cost can be turned into something redemptive if the Lord of all forgiveness frees our hearts.

Are you willing to take the responsibility? The first price to be paid here is the cost to look at yourself. Assume your part. Assume your responsibility. If you can do that, you can move into forgiveness.

That's His way of looking at reality. Name it. Acknowledge it to
somebody else. Take responsibility for it and then forgive. That's the only
way to bring life where there is no life.

We have spent significant time placing the parable of the
unforgiving steward in its context. Jesus precedes the parable with
a discussion of mutual accountability within Kingdom relationships.
Most of us cringe at the thought of confronting a brother who has
sinned against us (Mt. 18:15). It is equally difficult to be humble enough
to confess that we know we have wronged another (Mt. 5:23) and
need reconciliation before our worship of God can begin unhindered.
Responsibility before God goes in both directions. *Both the wronged and the
wrong-doer are accountable before God.* To see a speck clearly in another's eye
means I have to face all of the planks in my own (Mt. 7:3-5).

Treating one who has sinned against us as a person under the
judgment and grace of God, just as we are, includes the responsibility
of personal confrontation. There is pain in that prospect, but it also is
an ordained means of grace as well (Mt. 18:15b-20). To initiate such a
radical line of communication and Spirit-defined restoration is
impossible without knowing forgiving grace firsthand. There is a
divine cost long before any human price is paid. James Denney notes
that we need the entire gospel to understand the initiation of God in all
forgiveness. For God, "never requires anything He does not exhibit,
and that seeking love, which takes the initiative and is willing to
spend and be spent to the uttermost in the work of reconciliation, is
the breath of His being."[7] But the human side is inseparable from the
divine. And it must be done without resentment. As Denney says we,
"...must not grudge any self-humbling that is necessary to win the
offending brother."[8]

The cost of true, Christian forgiveness is clear for every person
involved. It costs to confront, to confess, to bear wrongdoing without

exacting retribution, and to face human brokenness in both the sinner and the sinned against.

> *(T)here is no such experience in the relations of human beings as a real forgiveness which is painless, cheap, or easy. There is always the passion in it on both sides: a passion of penitence on the one side, and the more profound passion of love on the other, bearing the sin of the guilty to win him, through reconciliation, to goodness again."*[9]

Do you have peace and joy in your spirit? Are you clean of all moral hindrances i.e., a sense of right and wrong by which you have limited grace toward anyone else? Are you honest about any unwillingness to relate at the heart level that the Lord might require of you? You can be clean in Him. He is present in the middle of chaos. Receive His grace and offer that received Life to those around you who need it so desperately.

[1] McGee *Search for Significance*, 318-31. *He mentions a couple more and draws some different definitions and conclusions but I am grateful for his main points.*

[2] Several of the major themes of this book and the phrase 'grievance debt collector' was first shared with me by my pastor during both college and seminary years, Dr. David Seamands. Over the years I have found that many of my colleagues at that time were deeply helped by his insightful counseling and preaching. See *Healing for Damaged Emotions* (Wheaton, IL: Scripture Press, 1981) and *Putting Away Childish Things* (Wheaton, IL: Scripture Press, 1983). It is also intriguing that later in his life after helping thousands deal with unforgiveness that he himself had to confess sin and receive the forgiveness he so beautifully exposited. Our need for grace never ends.

[3] From a sermon entitled, "It Shall Not be Forgiven," by George MacDonald in *Creation in Christ*, ed. Rolland Hein, (Wheaton, IL: Harold Shaw Publishers, 1976), 47-61.

[4] Mt 12:31-32, Mk 3:28-29, Lk 12:10

[5] Joyce Landorf,(now Heatherly,) *Irregular People* (Waco, TX: Word Publishing, 1982), 28-38.

[6] In my research I have been intrigued by the comparative paucity of references to forgiveness in the Early Church in comparison to our modern/postmodern preoccupation with it. There is an early connection between the ordained and the believer in terms of a mediation of absolution within the Body of Christ.See for example; third century, Roman theologian Hippolytus' *On the Apostolic Tradition* (Crestwood, NJ: St. Vladimir's, 2001), 61.

[7] Denney, *Christian Doctrine of Reconciliation*, 135. The entire discussion is very helpful. Ibid., 132-136.

[8] Ibid., 135.

[9] On this line of thought it is intriguing that Macintosh quotes Denney in his *Christian Experience of Forgiveness*, 190.

He was unwilling, however, but went and threw him in prison until he should pay back what was owed. So when his fellow slaves saw what had happened, they were deeply grieved and came and reported to their lord all that had happened. Then, summoning him, his lord said to him, "You wicked slave, I forgave you all that debt because you entreated me. Should you not also have mercy on your fellow slave even as I had mercy on you and his lord." And his lord, moved with anger, handed him over to the torturers until he should repay all that was owed him. So shall my heavenly Father also do to you, if each of you does not forgive his brother from your heart.

Matthew 18:30-35

6

The Costs
of a Forgiveness That Judges

But the painful fact will show itself, not less curious than painful, that
it is more difficult to forgive small wrongs than great ones. Perhaps
however, the forgiveness of the great wrongs is not so true as it seems.
For do we not think it a fine thing to forgive such wrongs and so do
it rather for our own sakes than for the sake of the wrongdoer? It is
dreadful not to be good, and to have bad ways inside one
George MacDonald *Annals of a Quiet Neighborhood*

AM I WILLING TO ASSUME THE COST TO FORGIVE?

We have been working with the idea that forgiveness costs the
forgiver everything. We must ask ourselves this profoundly disturbing
question: "Are we able to assume the cost of forgiveness as a judgment
of our own sin?"

Forgiveness is always a judgment of sin.

It is never a toleration of sin, never a glossing over of sin.

It is the only true way of looking at sin.

It is not indifference.

It is not condoning.

In fact, forgiveness often includes a punishment of sin.

We must never separate justice from self-giving love. Holiness and Love are co-equal realities in the Life of the Trinity. There is no discounting that fact when we look at the Incarnation and forgiveness. That judgment cost Jesus His life. To judge sin for what it is, always costs. I believe many times in my life I've been sinned against or I've sinned towards somebody else and I have actually forgotten that sin bears a judgment. For real health to be restored to a relationship every party involved must take a long, sober look at who they really are. Sin is always eternal until somebody takes care of it. That's what Jesus has done for us on the cross.

Our doctrine of the atonement must incorporate the fact that the cross was the forgiveness of God based upon the judgment of God for that sin. Sin is never just condoned by God. No sin is. God is not indifferent to sin – ever. And forgiveness is the proof of His seriousness in dealing with sin. Jesus is the forgiveness of God.

A Realistic Cost

Therefore, the first cost for forgiveness is a judgment of *realism*. We must realize how horrible sin is. There has to be radical honesty here. One of the first steps towards forgiveness is for us to desire to listen to the person who has wronged us. The first response of vindictive judgment can be another expression of self-protection. Notice how quickly your anger flairs or you lose self-control when you are wronged. Anger, like pain, serves many good uses but it can also be a barometer of mean-spiritedness.

There is an honesty offered by the Spirit in the communion of the saints which most of us never get close to. Not only do we need to be willing to respond to the sinner in patient forbearance, but we must also be willing to take the risk to speak to the wrong. For many it is a merely a vain hope to be able to openly communicate; to say to the wrongdoer, "Listen to me, you've hurt me here. I want you to hear me out - to get to the truth." That is realistic – and costly – judgment. And it is required by Jesus (Mt 18:15-17).

Anytime I have been that open with my wife, with my children, with my siblings, or with my parents, it has always been a costly situation. You can be misunderstood; you can be rejected. The judgment of honest dialogue is a rare experience. If you have ever known it, you are a blessed person. But let's consider, what is the full meaning of forgiveness? It surely is more than simply saying in our heart, "It's not that important, I'll just walk away." The truth is that we may walk away but the resentment does not. It stays between the injured and the wrong-doer, festering and infecting the relationship. Jesus didn't just walk away. He pointed at sin. He didn't tolerate any element of evil without speaking to its fundamental source. Please understand, with forgiveness there is the accompanying realistic cost of judging sin for what it is. And that judgment if directed towards everyone in a relationship broken by sin and needing forgiveness.

An Honest Appraisal of Who I Am

This judgment must start with the same spirit that produced the Incarnation and the Atonement; compassion that is willing to bear another's sin. And since, to be human means that we have sinned, we must start by judging ourselves. The real power of forgiveness begins to be seen when the hurt one judges himself or herself. It is to turn the spotlight back on our own hearts. It is interesting, even as I'm writing this, to realize that my default system is to condemn the wrongdoer when Jesus is really saying to all of us like Peter, "My friend, this is a problem in your heart." You must forgive from your heart first if there's going to be any forgiveness. So the cost of being real costs us our sense of rightness. It is never squeamish; it is always a confrontation that releases the ledger of justice.

It will cost us our sense of rage. It will cost us our sense of power. It may cost us our well-rehearsed victim status. Oh, we love being the victim. It makes us feel so good. It gives a sense of false security based upon power to be the one who has received wrong. All the judging goes only one way then, toward the one who has done something atrocious. But what a remarkable thing when Jesus so forgives us that we are released from a permanent victimization status.

We are no longer powerless. We are now in Christ - empowered to forgive and to change our lifestyles to no longer be a codependent victim of somebody else's wrongdoing toward us. It may cost us our sense of innocence. There may be some place in life where we are simply protecting ourselves from reality and the Lord is saying through this doctrine of forgiveness, "No, you need to move from perceived innocence into reality." There must be a place where you confront this. It may be that somebody is wronging someone else and you must stand in the middle of that and say, "No more." We are involved because forgiveness is a dynamic cost and a dynamic truth that we are willing to pay and to express.

Forgiveness costs us the plans of restoring relationship in any other way. If somebody has sinned against you, the only way back to relationship is through forgiveness. Not by counseling alone, not by tape series alone, not by listening to a radio message alone. It is only by saying

"Lord, I want to restore this relationship at whatever level you want me to restore it. Please make that possible."

I think most of us hold what people do against us in our hearts for a long time and we don't realize just how deep the damage penetrates. Consider this paragraph written by author Walter Wangerin: He says this about marriage but it can be applied to any relationship. The cost of forgiveness is this,

> *Forgiving will not immediately soothe your pain. Instead, it introduces a different pain. A much more hopeful pain because it is redeeming pain. You do deny yourself and die a little in order to forgive. Pride dies, fairness dies, rights die, as do self-pity and the sweetness of a pout, that or the satisfaction of a little righteous wrath. You take leave of the center of the marriage or the relationship and of your own existence. You die a little that the marriage might rise alive. You die a little that the relationship might rise again.*[1]

Isn't that interesting that there is can be no full relationship without death and resurrection? Every single person we have ever had a relationship with will need forgiveness and forgiveness always costs. It even costs you beyond pride, beyond fairness, beyond rights. It will cost you that sweet little pout at the end of a family disagreement where you've had to forgive.

I've lived with years of that sort of incomplete transaction in my own quiet time with the Lord, the unfulfilling 'satisfaction' of a little righteous wrath as I attempt to pray, keeping it, nursing it, justifying it. What a feeling of semi-deity to know that somebody else has done something against me and I can hold it in my own imperious rectitude. But forgiveness is not a numbers game. Forgiveness comprehends a grace that never holds, what Wangerin is painfully correct in adding, any pout against me. Therefore, I cannot hang on to any level of a little self-righteous wrath toward anyone. I must take leave of my resentment and I must die. If we forgive, we will die toward something – that is, a sense of our own righteousness or of arrogant judgment. It is always a life-threatening thing to forgive. It meant that for Jesus every time He spoke the word. It is no different for us who forgive in His Name.

What it Cost Jesus

If you think the cost for Jesus was miniscule, think again. When Jesus spoke this parable, you cannot miss that the shadow of the Cross permeates everything He said about forgiveness. Adam and Eve were clothed with animal skins. Abraham had to have a ram on Mt. Moriah. There would be no forgiveness without a sacrificial provision. There were millions of blood sacrifices in Israel's history as a daily reminder of the cost for every sin, unwitting or meticulously planned. Even Simeon's statement to Mary - *a sword will pierce your heart,* he says because she would watch forgiveness take place through her son's death. And, like us, forgiveness had to also occur in Mary's life. Jesus paid the price for all. Even His mother.

When Jesus comes to the man who is taken by his four friends down through a roof, he says, "Your sins are forgiven." How can He say that? It had meaning only because the shadow of the cross went over the house that day. In John 8, the woman is brought in adultery and she is not condemned any longer. Jesus lovingly commands, "Go and sin no more." Where would the power come from to actually confirm that statement? The reality was that He would pay the price for her adultery. She could not pay it. It is clear no other religious person around her cared one whit for her. Jesus would pay it and in this very beautiful and simple parable Jesus says you can be forgiven and you can forgive.

How do we know that? He has paid the price for all wrongdoing: what we have committed and that done toward us. For our wrong and their wrong, he has paid the cost. He took the judgment of all sin wrong into Himself. Holiness and love are equally revealed in the Son of Man. In "every great forgiveness there is enshrined a great agony."[2] Therefore, if I'm going to be a disciple of Jesus, I must also be willing to pay that price as well.

Forgiveness is a penetration of God's Life into a sinful world, a comprehension of divine grace. But here's where it gets hard: forgiveness is being willing to die to my own sense of rightness and to accept God's sense of rightness because of what he's done on my behalf. To relinquish the right to give what is deserved requires a passion of true love, a love that is holy.

Compassion incorporates passion. To ignore sin is not forgiveness because it does not involve pain. If no one suffers there is no forgiveness.[3] We de-personalize the sinner when we gloss over sin. If incarnation was required to forgive the sins of the world, then we are no less involved in the passion required to forgive. Forgiveness is much more powerful than forms of civility. "Such a (superficial) relationship between persons could obviously be no more than external and tolerantly civil; it would imply no communion of spirit, no pity, no love, no mutually interchange of inner feelings," as Macintosh keenly observes.[4] There is no bearing, no self-giving in political maneuvering. Niceties cloud true forgiving. Forgiveness incorporates all that we are in its healing stream. The cost of compassion touches every part of the one who gives themselves to Christ's method of restorative grace.

How does God make that kind of life real in the world? It's always costly to forgive because forgiveness is, the key penetration of His life into our sinful world. II Corinthians 5 says: He became sin for us. That is as penetrating as you can get. He came to our sin. He became like us in the sense that He took our sin upon Himself, though He was never sinful and redeemed it within himself. He paid our unrepayable debt.

Now, with that verse in II Corinthians 5 in mind let's put together the Lord's phrase in Matthew 6:12. As he teaches us to pray to our Heavenly Father, *forgive our sins as we forgive those who sin against us*. Now, surely the Lord does not mean here some kind of works righteousness. Surely, He does not mean that you and I are not forgiven unless we *do* forgiveness. To be like Jesus involves the passionate power to forgive the hard-hearted. That power does not come from apathy, cowardice or lethargy. This kind of love, "Demands my soul, my life, my all," as the famous hymn by Isaac Watts reminds us.[5]

I am a Protestant Christian who believes that Jesus gives forgiveness to us freely. Can he really be saying *I forgive your sins but you do something else entirely since you are only human?* What I think He's saying here in a much deeper level is, *we must do what He has done.* The key word in Matthew 6 is not "forgive"; the key word is "as".

Unless we forgive *as* He has, then there is no full understanding of His forgiveness. If we are to be forgiving agents in the world, then we realize something about what it means to be a Christian. Forgiveness is God's expression of His grace in the world and the only expression He has chosen that people can fully comprehend is living, breathing, human beings who have been freed in their lives of sin and now are paying the cost of forgiving everyone they know around them, no matter what happens to them.

To proclaim this to the abused, the damaged is no easy thing. To ask that a victim consider absorbing the sinner's sin and releasing them from vindictive judgment goes against the grain of logic, human conceptions of justice, and our demand for our rights. The only way that this can make sense is by looking to Jesus, the Author and Finisher of forgiveness. As in most theological dead-ends, our perception of the implications of forgiving grace becomes more of a preoccupation with ourselves than with becoming living sacrifices unto Him.

He understands the pain. He alone comes to the aid of the afflicted. He never misses a single sinful act. He will be the Judge of all. But before the King comes to settle accounts for the last time, He calls us to join Him. As the author of Hebrews encourages, "Let us, then, go to him outside the camp, bearing the disgrace He bore" (13:13 NIV). Paul Jensen is correct where he plumbs the depths of the costliness of forgiveness. He writes, "I doubt there is anything more difficult in all the world than exhausting in one's being the consequences of another's sin."[6]

Here it is plain, simple and shockingly stark.

If we are truly Christian and if He came forgiving, then we must turn around and pay the price of forgiving those around us.

It is an everyday thing - there will never be a day in which we don't have to forgive somebody, something.

And it will cost – just as it cost Him.

Identifying with the Wrong-doer

In the days of a one-room apartment, a pull-out sofa bed with a three inch mattress, no money to do anything but read to each other, my wife and I still remember with fondness G.K. Chesterton's *Father Brown Mysteries*. They are remarkable little stories. Some (for me, most) were so multi-faceted and deep that I didn't get the solution but I had to act like I did because Diane always did. I began to realize soon after we began reading to each other that one of the intriguing things about these mystery stories is that they were based upon the priest, Father Brown, who was able to take the mystery of the moment into his own mind and think, "What would I have done?"

What he was doing, basically, was what forgiveness often is. He was paying the price of identifying with somebody else's wrongdoing. There was a cost involved: the price of self-judgment. The priest-detective was actually saying, *You know I would be that person without the grace of God, I would have done that same thing.* So he was able to solve mysteries and bring about justice because he actually identified with the wrongdoer.[7]

It then struck me one day - *I wonder if that same spirit could change actual relationships?* If I was actually able to ask first, *if I had been in that situation, what would I have done?* If I had a spouse who wronged me, every single day, what sort of response would arise in my heart? I have learned never to react to overt expressions of anger due to those ruminations about others real circumstances. Maybe the teller who barked at me the bank counter has more going on in her life than meets the eye? What would I do if I were she? Could I have understood her enough to know that she was not specifically trying to hurt me? She simply was unable to respond appropriately because her life was totally a mess, totally painful.

To identify with somebody says, *I am not better than they are. I simply want to bring forgiveness as the first and most holy response.* To forgive is a realistic judgment of myself before I dispense anything to anyone. Huge tracks of pride are done away with if one is willing to enter into this cost of pardoning identification.

Forgiveness is, significantly, personal identification, a penetration into the world. If we simply bring power and punishment, then no one is changed. Forgiveness is the non-powerful divine potency that changes people's lives.

Sin is Not the Last Word

I remember vividly the day one of my theological mentors sat in a hotel dining room and shared with me an unforgettable story. My friend is John Cho, a marvelous preacher and equally brilliant teacher who subsequently led one of the largest seminaries in Asia. He serves on the pastoral staff of a huge church in Seoul, South Korea. He described the experience of a colleague whose wife and son were killed by the North Koreans in the Korean War. He garnered the debt of unconscionable outrageous criminality perpetrated against him and his entire family. His natural response was an all-consuming bitterness and rage.

Then an amazing thing happened. The soldier who had shot his loved ones was arrested on wartime criminal charges and Dr. Cho's friend was invited to the courtroom proceedings. Both he and those who accompanied him fully expected there to be a sweet sense of revenge. He looked at the face of the man who had viciously stolen the most precious people in his life from him. But as he looked at the darkened visage of this broken human being, waves of repulsion were displaced by a stronger surge of grace. It was an unexpected transaction. A divine exchange. Reflecting upon that grace-filled encounter he stated, *I refused that morning by the grace of Jesus to continue the rage. I could stop there.* And he did. He forgave the murderer. The man paid the full price for his crime but the living victim released him.

That's what we need – refusing, by the grace of Jesus, to embrace and retain the bitterness. You see, this man comprehended divine grace but he also paid a cost; the cost of saying this next sentence. *Sin is not going to have the last word, even the sin of the murder my wife and son.* This marvelous Christian man was given a heart enough like Jesus to say, *The last word in this is not going to be sin, or self, or bitterness. The last word in this is not going to be my human sense of justice.* And as that decrepit soul passed him, with deep pain in his eyes, the victim's family member responded by saying: *I forgive you for what you've done.*

The Hurter Hurts Worse than the Hurted

When my wife and I were engaged one of the first persons I wanted to share our joy with was the man who had discipled and loved me for years.

Upon presenting ourselves, he said "Bill, remember that the hurter always hurts worse than the hurted." I was so flummoxed by what seemed to me to be rain on my nuptial parade, that to this day I don't remember what I thought he really meant. But in the years since then, nearly every time someone has done something wrong to me, the Spirit has brought back that sentence and I have been able to think about reality as it is found in the Lordship of my forgiving King, Jesus Christ.

Maybe you are like me at this point of shameful confession. I have always liked it when somebody has done something wrong to me because it makes me feel better is a distorted way. *I'm not so bad. They are the bad guy.* No. Remember that the hurter always hurts worse than your experience of hurt. The reason why they feel more pain is because of their own sin. They hurt out of deep shame and a crushing sense of inadequacy.

While we might not know why they do harmful things, if we respond by the penetration of God's life in the world we can say like our Korean brother, *sin is not going to have the last word.* My sense of righteousness is not the last word. My first and last word is grace. Grace is Jesus fully revealed in my life by the Holy Spirit. I have received Him and thus I've received grace. I am receiving it and, therefore, God's life is going to respond to that sin in radical grace. I'm going to incarnate, by the power of the Spirit, God's life in the world. Could that be why we repeat so often these words:

Forgive our sin, Jesus, as we forgive those who have sinned against us?

He breaks the power of cancelled sin, but you and I must endure the consequence and overcome our resentment. We live too easily and too freely with our resentment.

Did Jesus really mean it when He said, *If you are my disciple, you must take up your cross and follow me?* I fear that our underlying response is more along the lines of, "Yes, but He meant that exclusively for those going into the ministry, like the mission field or working in a Christian organization. Following Him could not mean actually taking sin into myself? That is taking identifying with Jesus' view of sinners way too seriously."

No, it is a serious thing to follow Jesus. He said what He means. He has paid the price for everyone involved in every sinful occurrence. And it cost Him everything to do so. You must also be willing to exhaust the sin done against you as you take it into yourself. God says *I'll take care of the ultimate result of that sin. You expunge it. Finish it. You finish it by your willingness to offer the grace with which I have filled your life; no grace and be offered except for that which you received from Me.*

Is His forgiveness penetrating your life today? It will as you judge sin – in your life and others. But this also means penetrating the world in which you literally live day by day with His life that is so self-dispensing that it takes sin in and melts it by redeeming love.

He has paid the price.

We must also. Let that person who has sinned against you go in His name.

There is nothing more freeing in the world.

---

[1] Walter Wangerin Jr. *As For Me and My House* (Nashville: Thomas Nelson, 1990), 95-96

[2] Macintosh, Christian *Experience of Forgiveness*, 218.

[3] Denney, *The Christian Doctrine of Reconciliation*, 135.

[4] See this and a similar idea throughout Macintosh's brilliant analysis of the pain in real forgiveness in *The Christian Experience of Forgiveness*, 31. He notes that the "The Bearer of forgiveness perishes." Ibid., 101. He places Bushnell in a favorable light who wrote that true forgiveness requires both a, "sympathy with the wrong-doing party as *virtually takes on his nature*; and secondly, *a making cost in that nature by suffering*." Ibid., 188. He quotes A. G. Hogg who asserts, "There is in the holiness of God a radical opposition to wickedness which cannot express itself adequately in mere punishment, but can express itself *only by receiving upon itself the assault of the sinful will*," Ibid., 202. Italics added for emphasis. See also, 216-219.

[5] Isaac Watts, "When I Survey the Wondrous Cross," *Hymns and Spiritual Songs*, 1707.

[6] Paul Jensen, "Forgiveness and Atonement," *Scottish Journal of Theology*, 46: 159. Jensen's responses to philosophical challenges to the nature of forgiveness are succinct and helpful. His perspective underscores the ideas in this chapter which necessitate that God Incarnate had to take into His own being the sin of the world in order for either the atonement or forgiveness to have any real meaning or transformative power. He is clear on the volitional nature of both the Incarnation and the Triune God's willing inclusion of sin into His unchanging nature by the work on the cross.

[7] See for example the statement when asked how he could know how a murdered thought about his victim: "I am a man," answered Father Brown gravely; "and therefore have all devils in my heart." Found in G. K. Chesterton, *The Complete Father Brown* (Harmondsworth, England: Penguin Books, 1987), "The Eye of Apollo," 130. See also ibid., 465-466, "I *am* inside a man. I am always inside a man, moving his arms and legs; but I wait till I know I am inside a murderer, thinking his thoughts, wrestling with his passions; till I have bent myself into the posture of his hunched and peering hatred; till I see the world with his bloodshot and squinting eyes, looking between the blinkers of his half-witted concentration; looking up the short and sharp perspective of a straight road to a pool of blood. Till I am really a murderer."

> *Then, summoning him, his lord said to him, "You wicked slave, I forgave you all that debt because you entreated me. Should you not also have mercy on your fellow slave even as I had mercy on you and his lord." Moved with anger, he handed him over to the torturers until he should repay all that was owed him. So shall my heavenly Father also do to you if each of you does not forgive his brother from your heart.*
>
> Matthew 18:32-35

7

The Discovery that Breaks the Cycle

Some ancient ascetic writers recommended a practice whose most famous
recent exponent is Chesterton's Father Brown: entering imaginatively into
the heart of every kind of criminal, knowing that that criminal is oneself;
finding the murderer, the blackmailer, the thief in oneself.

Simon Tugwell, *Prayer*

FORGIVENESS IS A DISCOVERY

At the beginning of this book we summarized one of the most
riveting stories of the twentieth century. Simon Wiesenthal's experience
has been the subject of endless discussions on ethics and the meaning of
evil. But in the same period of time in the concentration camp named
Ravensbruck, a Dutch woman and her sister were enduring atrocities
similar to those described in *The Sunflower*. Corrie ten Boom watched

her beloved sister die a slow and painful death in that camp. She had every reason to be bitter at the unspeakable horrors of the torturous hours spent in captivity. But in the midst of what most of us would argue was only a struggle for survival, Corrie was attuned enough to that which was real and true to discover something about herself.

It began with her rationalizing that keeping food for her sick sister alone was right when all around her there were starving women. She confessed that it was her weaker sister, Betsie, who encouraged her to share an extra blanket with a new inmate for the freezing nights. She judiciously meted out 'help' but it was not from a heart of love. There was always the expectation of an immediate return. With every reason to cry out against the injustice of inhumane sadism Corrie began to be confronted by the 'cancer' in her own soul. It is amazing how like the 'unjust steward' we all are at base until we come face to face with our abject inability to live the Life of Unreserved Grace that is our King's alone to give. Jesus alone is the Life of Self-Disposing Love in the Spirit to the glory of the Father. There is no limit of suffering to which He will not go to make His blessings known.

Corrie was set free from her 'self', but it had to be uncovered by the Holy Spirit and discovered through her absolute ruthlessness with her own heart even in the midst of what most of us would consider righteous indignation. When one is so mistreated, is not stone-like indifference the way to stay alive? After the War was over and she returned to Holland she found that many people could not forgive. They simply re-played all the old wrongs in either silent rage or endless grumbling. She described post-war people as mirroring the cities of rubble with, "minds and hearts of ashes."[1]

But Corrie herself had to face her own demons in order to discover what Jesus truly wanted to do in a full identification with His sufferings. At the end of a meeting, one of the SS guards who had stood by as Betsie and Corrie had participated in the camp's horrific humiliations came up to her expecting a response of total acceptance because he could claim with her the grace of Jesus for all sin. He extended his hand seeking a symbol of restored fellowship, of forgiveness. Corrie tightened, not sure what was right to do to this former Nazi complicit in the deaths of nearly a 100,000 women. Her prayer is one we all must learn. If you have not received grace you cannot give it. Forgiveness costs everything. Forgiveness is a discovery of who I am and Who He Is.

She recounts that she felt no emotion whatsoever, but she breathed these words, "Jesus, I cannot forgive him. Give me Your forgiveness." What happened next she could only compare with an electrical current as she experienced a love that she could never have elicited on her own springing up like an Artesian well within her. Overwhelmed by the reality of the power of self-giving love she recounts the theology of her discovery in this way, "(I)t is not on our forgiveness any more than on our goodness that the world's healing hinges, but on His. When He tells us to love our enemies, He gives, along with the command, the love itself."[2]

We can release a person in forgiveness but often there are other tentacles that hang on that need to be honestly dealt with. Further conversation, discussion and honesty which abolish any moral hindrance to fellowship with a wrongdoer and reestablish the freedom and happiness of a healthy relationship. We do not give what a person deserves and give them what they do not deserve apart from forgiving grace – willingness, and openness to further communication. All of these put an end to de-personalizing hatred and serve to re-personalize both ourselves and the one who sinned against us.

Notice the word is *willingness* to open up choked channels of relational reciprocity. We do not in any way guarantee relationship by forgiving. It is never a simple operation. We merely open up ourselves to being made willing to have that relationship restored. I believe many of us can forgive, but we sure don't want to go back into the relationship. We have more lines of barriers than most actual battlefields. Forgiveness is not a dis-covering of our true nature and the truer reality of transforming grace until we are willing to be uncovered for who we really are and then say, "Jesus, whatever you say, I will do it. I want you to be glorified. I want you to be the one in charge of this relationship, not me."

How is forgiveness is a discovery? If I am willing to keep my heart bigger than any offense and harbor no judgmental attitude then:

I'm discovering something about myself.

I'm discovering that I now have an honest appraisal of sin.

I'm discovering that my sense of rightness is now done away with.

All sense of rage, of hate, of power, of pride, of victimization, all those things are gone.

I'm discovering that now I have in my life no other plan of relational restoration.

Forgiveness is the foundation but it is not the end. Forgiveness is the beginning of what we are to discover. We can talk about judgment, about cost, about the penetration of life in the world, but the Lord is taking us into a full identification with Himself. Forgiveness is not just being saved from the consequence of a sin. It is not merely a judicial release from God's judgment. It is always other-oriented. Forgiveness does not find its completion unless the divine nature begins working in the human heart to do away with any moral hindrance to relationship. That means nothing can be done to me in this life where I've said okay, that's it. That person is dead to me. While there are many heinous sins that require levels of security if there is going to be any form of further relationship, that is not the case with most sins done against us in daily life. A rape or a murder is not the same as a slander or a defrauding. It may not be clear at first but each of us have to deal with the spirit which states unequivocally, "Don't come near me again. I am never going to let you into my life in any way.

It is one thing to say that God comes to us in forgiveness but then we stop short of the clear command in Scripture that indicates that we too must forgive. All too often we make forgiveness an idea without a body, a presence. We lack a willingness to allow the Spirit to dictate the parameters of life in the process of forgiveness.

What if the wrongdoing is simply too wicked to countenance a re-entry into relationship? I'm thinking of those who may be living in an abusive situation. You may need to be physically apart from someone who is able and willing to hurt you. But, enabled by the power of the Holy Spirit, you have the choice to lay aside all moral reservations that threaten the full work of God in the relationship. The Holy One comes to all of us and says, *Even though you have been immoral, I will forgive you and now make you moral.* He never rejects any of us and, therefore, I cannot claim to be exceptional, to be unwilling to express that kind of moral love and grace in the world. It has to happen if the forgiveness of Jesus is to be the atmosphere of the Body of Christ and the aroma it offers to the world. That willingness must happen first in the heart.

Three Tests of Forgiveness and a Fourth

Here is a three-point test of forgiveness.[4]

First: The Test of *Resentment*. Just think, if you will, about the people in your life, with whom or by whom you have garnered a whole basket of resentment. Is there anybody in your life, anywhere, as far back as you can remember against whom you have held resentment almost all of your life? It is a shocking realization when that level of honesty exposes accumulated burdens of non-forgiven acts of sin.

If you have forgiven fully, you will be able to say, "I don't resent anyone. It's gone. Jesus has taken care of it. I still have feelings. I still remember. I still think about it from time to time, but the agonizing destructive force of unrequited justice, of resentment is gone. There is no moral hindrance there. Resentment is not present in my life as a debilitating cancer of my mind and heart."

Second: The Test of *Responsibility*. Have you been willing to take any responsibility for the sin done in your life? Like Peter we assume the other has sinned against us. Like him, we usually do not start with ourselves before God. Am I willing to actually say, "I forgive" to the place where I am willing to look at my own heart and say clearly, "You know, I was a part of that sin. I enabled it. I was codependent. I was seeking something I should not have sought for." Living with unabashed openness to the responsibility we have in each of our relationships is crucial to maintaining humility. And it is a witness to God's restorative power.

I find a deeper heart level of forgiveness when I see the Lord pointing back to me and saying, *Bill, you kept this problem relationship going by your own lack of claiming responsibility.* I believe forgiveness is a discovery, not so much about the other person, but about me, my heart.

Third: The test of *Reminders*. Have I been willing to let go of any way of holding on to an offense. Is there any place in my life where I have kept a reminder of that sin in my life? Is there a letter or a picture or any other symbol of that tragic occurrence? We can keep physical reminders but more often we keep emotional ones. Anger-filled reactions to comments made by others or shutting down emotionally when a person is mentioned are examples of non-physical retention of hostility toward another. It is hard place to go but we must ask ourselves, *Is there any person, any situation that I keep as a reminder of past wrongdoing? Am I willing to let the Holy Spirit free me of that reminder?*

A Triune Redemption

The fourth element of this test is the key and it is *redemption.* Have you been redeemed? I often hear sportscasters throwing the word 'redemption' around. I wonder if they have any idea what the theological foundation of that term is. To be redeemed is to be lifted out of a negative, even hopeless, situation and to be placed in an entirely different context. Col. 1:13 offers a powerful picture of this truth. Paul testifies that we have been rescued from a kingdom of darkness and 'transported' into the realm of the Kingly reign of the Son who is loved of the Father.

Behind the inheritance we have as children of God there is a divine deliverance. That is the only solution to the fact that we were under the power (*exousia*) of darkness. The Father and the Son took our self-induced bondage and broke its power through redemptive love. Darkness is not just the absence of what is true, it is defiant opposition; it is a usurping dominion. As our hearts resonate with the mythic power of this truth in the novels we read and the films we watch, the ones that point to the reality of our Redeemer's glorious emancipation.

Paul explores the positive nature of this deliverance in a unique way. He uses a term that we might make too theologically solemn. Note first the clarity of a focus on the Triune God; the "He" distinctly refers to the Father. It is in the eternal heart of the Three-in-One that the cycle of stultifying enslavement is broken. Let this powerful reality sink in to your heart:

He has *carried you* over into the promised land of His Life,

He has *transferred* (another power term!) you into the reign of His Love,[5]

He has *transported you* today, right here, right now into His Kingdom,

He has *translated you* into the same relationship He has with the Son of His Love,

He has *freed you* from a rebel kingdom and has brought you into the home which is your inheritance, the rulership of His beloved Son.

Note that we have switched one kingdom for another Kingdom! Where there was nothing but bondage and destruction there is now a context of mutuality that draws its life from the very heart of God. No hint of reservation, or shame need exist on either side of this deliverance. The deceptiveness of unforgiven sin is replaced by the glorious light of redeeming love, the Kingdom of the Son of His love.6 The context is one where there is life with others who love Jesus, in whom there is no darkness at all. That means that being one in the holy love between Father and Son in the Spirit is a constant source of receptivity. We receive that love in Him and through Him. In Him we have been made fit (1:12), rescued (1:13), transported (1:13) and in Him we have, or possess, redemption (1:14). Transporting and being ransomed are two vibrant pictures of the work of the King. These are unrepayable actions.[7] Our deliverance is in Him; being in union with Him.

Israel's self understanding had always been that God brought them out and made them His own. So for the believer in Christ, "In Him" is saying that in Him alone we find redemption, release, pardon. The believer is the one who is found in Him. But note that the ransoming must also work itself out as a remission. Paul concludes, or maybe, climaxes the litany of liberation with "the forgiveness of sins."[8]

If you've been redeemed, you can offer redemption to other people. Of course, it's His life, it's His work, it's His grace, and it is His billion-dollar debt removed. Forgiveness is impossible apart from the grace of God.[9]

Are you truly living in the redemption of God? Is it so vibrant and real that you are offering His redemption through your yielded and selfless life?

The Levels of Communication

I have had the privilege to read a lot of books. I have found that there are some that have etched themselves into my life, while others may have increased knowledge but they have not formed the way I approach life. One book that left an indelible imprint on me was John Powell's *Why Am I Afraid to Tell You Who I Am?* Powell helped me to ascertain the various levels of communication in my relationships. I am still shocked by the accuracy of his assessment and how much of our lives can be squandered in non-transparent discourse.[10]

Powell begins this discussion by saying that most people spend their lives expressing themselves at the *level of cliché*. We all use common courtesies such as: "How are you doing?", or "Good morning" or, "Have a good day". These are not bad in themselves it is just that they we don't plumb anything beyond the surface. We are civil but carefully distant. We want to get along but we devise ways to avoid the necessity of self-giving. I have never had the nerve to respond to these questions with, "Do you really want to know how my day is? I will need an hour but if you truly want to know how I am that is what it would take." Clichés are like euphemisms. They are ways to not say anything that causes a ruckus. They are safety barriers.

If you have friends at school or work, ones you might have invited into your home from time to time, you probably share *facts and reports* with them. That's Powell's second level of communication. Normally, men talk about work or sports and women talk about relationships, recipes, fashion or family issues. Nothing much is invested at this level. Mere facts, by themselves, do little to accommodate intimacy.

If you have a good friend, you probably experience the third level of communication which is *opinions*. That's the beginning of real risk because when you share your opinions, you open up the possibility of disagreement. This means that you are vulnerable to the immediate opportunity for criticism if you share at this level. Opinions or opinionated people produce difficulty in relationships.

There is a fourth level which very few people engage in because they don't want to risk it. This is the place where we actually *judge right and wrong* and discuss why we believe something is seriously amiss or wonderfully good. Just try speaking about a common sin in our culture as a moral evil at the next dinner party you attend and see if you are invited back. We avoid judgments like the plague. The dark side of our addiction to tolerance is that now the only wrong thing is thinking something is actually wrong. Judgments are costly because they are self-revealing. Most of us have drawn the line of communication long before we get to this level.

Clichés, Facts and Reports, Opinions maybe, but Judgments? In our toleration-oriented society few of us are free to express that level of deep communication. We all draw an invisible line there. Judgments are avoided nearly at all costs. But we have to push through those barriers if there is ever going to be real communication and, thus, freedom from our insidious levels of self-protection.

Powell's exploration of the surface-level communication is withering if one looks at the amount of time actually spent on the lowest shelves of personal engagement. As I look at people who I would call friends, I would say that the first four are the most common levels that fill the majority of ordinary life. The more self-giving a level is the more intimate friendship becomes. But Christian life challenges every place we erect self-protecting barriers. It confronts facades with brave and selfless communication. Most of us want to love in true self-expression. But when we face the hard work resident in love and communication, we normally defer to the easier terms of opinions and reports and clichés. Maybe, on a good day if one is feeling really brave, we might offer a judgment or two. But the Bible offers us the *discovery of a deeper level of communication*.

By divine grace, believers are enabled to communicate at a substantive level that people apart from that goodness and mercy cannot truly share in. Relating to one another while drawing upon the Triune God as the source of all words (and the intentions behind them) places our mere 'puffs of air' on a whole new plane of communication.

First, is that we can communicate *affirmation* and truly mean it. "I affirm you because I love you freely," not calculating what we may or may not receive back. This is doubly difficult because there are many who can't receive the fact that the Lord affirms them. But with the Holy Spirit's self-giving comfort we discover we are able to affirm for truly selfless reasons. Imagine the freedom of affirming because we want to build the other person up, not tear them down. This ministry of blessing another life may not be possible person to person due to the trail of damage left by abusive sin. But it can be offered as a result of a heart that is released from bitterness and which desires God's righteousness and mercy to be displayed in the offender's heart.

Second, we are open to discovering that we can be rebuked. It's interesting that in Chapter 18 of Matthew, Peter's discussion with Jesus and the subsequent parable occur after the paragraph that says if a brother has sinned, you are to go and confront him. It's in the context of rebuke that Jesus gives this parable, yet many Christians are unable or unwilling to discover the level of their need of rebuke. They go through life with opinions and actions that frequently hurt others, saying and doing wrong things - and there is no one in their life that can hold them accountable for their cruel judgments and divisive deeds.

They are totally "unrebuke-able." They are "unentreatable."

I love the word entreat. Both servants *entreated* another (Mt 18:29,32). The one servant entreated the king, the other servant entreated his unforgiving co-worker. 'Entreated' means to open to something, to reveal one's heart. It is a sobering fact, however, that if you are transparent, someone will let you know that you are not as good as you think you are. It's hard for me to hear that criticism, but gives the necessary perspective to keep us from the much deeper pain that sin produces. To be "rebuke-able" breaks down the dam of self-protection and allows grace to flow through my heart to others.

This is a level of communication that few attempt, and apart from grace, it can be very painful, even destructive. That is why Jesus states that He must be where two or three are gathered in such a potentially volatile situation. In Christian communication we must go there very cautiously, but it is necessary level for real spiritual growth. I often ask people who their best friend is. When I press for the answer, it is almost always the person who loves them enough to challenge them with truth and accountability.

Third, we discover something about the heart of God. Forgiving communication reveals to us His character. Indeed, the end of forgiveness is not justice but the full nature of God. The servant in this parable saw only himself. And that is why, in the face of glorious goodness he responded out of fear. He allowed the anger of the king to be the sole controlling basis of his actions. His immediate attempt to pay back the king is an indication of living life based on a 'starkly humanistic' reading of forgiveness. The heart breaking reality is that many come away from Jesus' teaching as found in this parable and say, "Well, that's all we need. All we need is somebody to forgive us our debt. Now my life will be lived out of my ability to manipulate."

No. That is not the gospel that Jesus both is and offers.

This fellow was not changed. Nothing changed in him. If anyone is going to truly forgive, it must be more than simply a statement of God's justice. It's going to be the incursion of God Himself into our world; the character of God, His holiness, expressed in our actual lives. Forgiveness, if it does not change us at the heart level, is damaging to us and thus to others near us as this parable unflinchingly records. Jesus did not come simply to forgive us. He came because He wants to turn us into those who live like Himself. Forgiveness, you see, has to accentuate God's character.

Forgiveness is one of the clearest expressions of His character in the world. As stated previously, it may be the first place where anyone truly initiates a true conception of God. Forgiveness is not a sham. It is not a cover up. It is the truest response to sin. The distinctiveness the Christian doctrine of forgiveness is that Jesus Christ identifies with us on the cross so that we might become like Him. We forgive - why? Not because we know it is the right thing to do, not because it makes us feel better. We forgive so that others can become like Him.

For years, I thought, "Okay Lord, I'll get this grace thing down and then I'll forgive people and life will be better." In that narrow perspective lay my own defeat. Anyone who has tried to forgive in their own power without the continual access to the heart of God made available to us by the Spirit Himself knows the hopelessness of that agenda. The life of forgiveness is the nexus, the intersection where the character of the Holy One and the needs of people around us meet. As Isaiah said of the Messiah and sins, "they meet together in Him (Is 53:6). The forgiver comes to "bear" the sin of the world in union with the Savior. Only He can save but He only does so through us. There is no other reason for Jesus to tie divine forgiveness and our forgiveness together inseparably.

His ultimate purposes for all who are pardoned have never changed. We forgive ultimately so that other people can become like Him. We want the one who has pained us, the one who has sinned against us, to be like Jesus. If His forgiveness is the avenue of changing my heart, then maybe my forgiveness is the means for somebody else not to become like me, but become like Him.

Only by true forgiveness is that kind of character ever discovered. Pardon paves the way for purity. Justification is followed by sanctification. The door to the house of fellowship with God may be repentance and faith but the place of true relationship is the warm living area of holiness of heart and life.[11]

You might remember that General Oglethorpe, the man who brought John Wesley over to Georgia, in austere pomposity said, I *never forgive sins that are done against me* - apparently he carried a bit of self-righteous indignation, although he was an effective missionary in many ways. John Wesley, quipped back, *Well, General, then you better not ever sin.* If you're never, ever going to be able to forgive somebody, then you better make sure you never sin. Anyone reading this who thinks they've never sinned, has some deep problems. And if you bear any unforgiveness in your heart, then you have effectively cut off the supply lines of grace into your own soul.

If you move beyond the level of resentment, take responsibility, remove all reminders, and then accept the implications of redemption, you can take your life and make it a communication of true Christian depth. You can affirm. You can be rebuked and can discover the Life of God expressed in the world.

Incursion of God's Life in the World

Without a doubt the God-Man is speaking the parable (Matt 18:21-35) to reveal the very heart of God. Only the One who was going to pay the price for the debt all sin incurred could speak with such authority on the matter. The world into which He came was no different than ours, spiritually-speaking. There are, as it were, 'sectors' of the gospels that deal with forgiveness specifically concentrated:

at the beginning of Jesus' ministry,

near the pivot in the Savior's life from ministry to the cross,

and in the passion/resurrection narratives.

Those concentrations of this topic are not accidental. Forgiveness heralds the Life of God. It is a vanguard of all that He has to offer. And that may be exactly why the command to forgive is so inescapably given to us.

Something has to confront the hopelessness of the world without Christ. I remember reading years ago a comment that when one forgives the balance of the power of the universe shifts a bit. That author understood the profound supernatural significance of pardon. Otherwise we are left in the self-centered stupor of the steward in this parable. Sin committed becomes a part of the unmovable machine we call the "world." It is opposed to God, to life, to real joy and peace. Without release from sin we are chained to what Hannah Arendt calls, "relentless automatism."[12] Forgiveness breaks the power of that which shackles every heart and every relationship – guilt. It is the avenue through which every receptive heart can see the face of God.

Let me end this chapter with a helpful list of steps of restorative forgiveness which has been shared with me several times over my years of walking with Jesus. It was originally composed by the famed Korean evangelist Billy Kim. I came into possession of a guide called "The Guidelines to a Love Explosion." Taking all this theological discussion, seriously forced me to apply what the Word was calling me to both be and do. I began to actually employ this list in various circumstances and it assisted me in breaking down de-personalizing barriers, confronting deep-seated resistances in my own heart, as well as enabling me to forgive when I felt I had been wronged. Forgiveness as an explosion of love should take on skin. When I have followed these practices even for a few days, I find my entire outlook changes toward the wrongdoer and so does my relationship in the Spirit with them.

Billy Kim writes,

- First, read I Corinthians 13 for seven days in a row…read that chapter, the love chapter, seven days in a row with no one else in mind but the one who has wronged you.
- Second, pray for that person for seven days. Don't talk about the sin. Don't bring up the sin. Just simply pray for that person.
- Third, say nothing negative about that person for seven days.
- Fourth, refuse any negative thought about that person for the week. Pray" Holy Spirit, dispel any negativity. I'm not going to have that. I'm going to think about this person in light of I Corinthians 13 and I'm going to pray for their best in you. I want Your life in their life."
- Fifth, enumerate as many positives as possible about that person. There may not be many. There may only be one. But there has got to be at least one. Think about that thing. Dwell on that positive. Let that positive permeate your mind. Pray for God's best in their life.
- Sixth, listen with interest or compassion to someone who is extremely self-centered. This is close to our concept of discovery. Letting somebody else into your life that is as self-centered as you may have become due the wrong done to you can be

quite illuminating. If I'm listening to somebody who is really bothersome or preoccupied with self-pity, then maybe I can comprehend why the original infraction occurred. This is a great way of leveling out, of identifying with sin, and saying I forgive because, without divine grace in my life, I would have done the same thing.

- And last, do a good deed each day for seven days on the behalf of the person you don't like. Write a note. Send a card. Buy a lunch. Offer an affirmation on the way past them in the hall. Whatever it might be, stroke that person in a sweet kind of way for seven days and see what results in your heart.

Those of us who think that list appears easy to accomplish are not living close to reality. Most likely, the 'sin' done against you has not been a serious thing. I can remember when I said to myself - *Oh, it'll be easy.*

But then I lived a little while.

It's not so easy. In fact, all forgiveness is impossible without being first forgiven by God.

What I experienced was an incursion of God's life into relationships that I never knew possible before.[13] I noticed a change in my heart attitude toward my "irregular people," which Joyce Landorf calls those folks who can't see love, can't hear, or feel, or speak it. As I began to pray every day for the two main figures causing carnage in my life and as I read I Corinthians 13 over their lives, I began to realize how truly self-centered I was and I began to look at the Lord's Prayer in a whole different way. I've never been able to say it since then in the same way since then.

Forgive us our debts, as we forgive our debtor, became a very serious line to me. As a result of my study, I saw it as as the key phrase in that marvelous prayer to connect me with the world. Everything else in that prayer is about what I get. That one petition pertains to what I ought to be doing in response to the expressions of grace all around my life.

Think about this – out of all the biblical words for salvation in Scripture, in many of the major creeds in the Christian church that have been accepted over the centuries the word "forgiveness' was the term chosen by the early church fathers. Could it be that they saw forgiveness as the window into the life of God? At the base of all salvation is an expression of gracious pardon that 'leads' to everything else.[14]

Not justification. Not sanctification. But forgiveness.

Why? It certainly is not that they don't care about those other concepts. What they are saying is that if we understand forgiveness, then we will discover who God really is; and if we are forgiven, then we might be able to uncover our own self-centered lives towards somebody else. We can discover why they sinned. We can discover why they are in pain, and we can discover ourselves in love toward them. We can forgive. We can give life because He is our Life.

Do you have a great dream in your heart about doing something wonderful for Jesus? Let me tell you the first place where you can change the world: you can change it by forgiving someone near you.

I came across a story several years ago of a man in ministry was having a difficult time with his wife. One night he pounded the table and raged at his wife, *I hate you. I won't take it anymore. I've had enough. I won't go on. I won't let it happen. No. No. No.* And, several months later, walking down the hallway passing just outside his two year old son's bedroom door, he heard in a soft, yet strained voice, with perfect inflection, imitating the fierce anger, those same words: *I hate you. I won't take it anymore. No. No. No.*

Could you break the cycle of unforgiveness in your life today with somebody? If not, somebody other than you is paying the price. I believe we can discover the Life of God if we forgive like He forgives. Is there anyone, anywhere toward whom you are holding resentment? Can the Holy Spirit release you today? Is there any place where there is a reminder of that sin against you in your life?

Give it to the Holy Spirit. Let Him touch it. The Lord wants to take us somewhere behind and beyond forgiveness. If we could just forgive, then maybe we could discover the Life of God in our life. He turns us into forgivers who reveal the very heart of God.

[1] Corrie ten Boom, *The Hiding Place* (Minneapolis, MN: Chosen Books, 1971), 233.

[2] Ibid., 233.

[3] The necessary place of 'boundaries' is a relatively new discipline in the dynamics of Christian relationships. All that I have read and heard sounds very insightful and mostly helpful. My concern here is mostly directed toward what I sense is the 'over' application of sound concepts. A boundary can become self-protective in an impregnable way and that does not seem to be at all what Jesus was teaching his disciples at any point. At the risk of sounding naïve I think we need the distinct leading of the Holy Spirit in guarding against abuse while yielding ourselves to the risk of relationship that the forgiveness we have received from Jesus is mirrored in our actual lives. He does not lay down any barrier except that the sinner repent and return to Him. In a mysterious way the graced life should image the Savior in similar extension of unreserved graciousness.

[4] I found some of these words on a scrap of paper from some sermon notes taken during my college days. Eitherthey came from Dr. David Seamands or from another of the giants of faith that blessed my life during those days at Asbury College or the Wilmore (KY) United Methodist Church. My life has been surfeited by grace and truth.

[5] 9t. the NT refers to the kingdom of Christ ex. Lk 23:42, Rev 1:9

[6] This is the only time Paul uses this particular phrase in relation to the Father and the Son. The translation, 'His dear Son' loses the power of the phrase. The Early Church interpreters made much of the genitive making much of the option of a genitive of origin. Several church fathers mention this as a probable reference to the intra-trinitarian mutuality; the Son begotten in love by the Father for eternity. Regardless, Paul is aware that the Son and the Father has always been , in love. This love is affirmed throughout Gospel, Mt3:17, Lk. 9:35.

[7] The basic term for redemption in Greek is *'lutron'*, here *apolutrosis*, a release from, or something paid so that I could go free. Main focus is emancipation but it is based upon a price paid, ex. Mk 10:45 *he gave his life a ransom for many* and I Tim 2:6 *a ransom for all.* Paul, as we, have to fight to keep idea of substitution in force. Nothing of our salvation lies in us.

[8] Here forgiveness is the translation of *aphesis*: Paul uses it only elsewhere at Eph 1:7, which means, 'to send away' sin, (we have noted Ps. 103:12; Micah 7:19; Is. 43:25;44:22 which tell us how far He sends sin away),' to release from a debt,' and 'to free from guilt'. It is also interesting that Paul uses *aphiemi* in only one context where it can clearly be translated as forgiveness. Cf. his use in Rom. 4:7 in comparison with I Cor 7:11-13 where it is used for divorce.

[9] A dear teacher and friend of mine, Dr. David Thompson has produced one of the most helpful books on relational healing I have ever read. *His Holiness for Hurting People* (Indianapolis: Wesleyan Publishing, 1998) has a short but poignant section of 'authentic forgiveness.' Fundamentally, all forgiveness is impossible apart from the saving grace of God in Christ. Ibid., 142-144.

[10] John Powell, *Why Am I Afraid to Tell You Who I Am?* (Niles, Il: Argus Communications, 1969), 50-62. Powell's levels are enumerated differently to lead to the inner most sharing of one's heart: 5. Cliché 4..Reporting the facts about others, 3. My ideas and

judgments , 2. My feelings, emotions, and 5, what Powell calls "peak Communication" but I am adding some further insights here.

[11] I am grateful for the theology of John Wesley which is redolent in the words of this paragraph.

[12] Hannah Arendt, *The Human Condition* (Chicago: University of Chicago Press, 1959), 216. This is a phenomenal piece of philosophy which merits close study. Arendt's sophisticated argument hold forgiveness out as the only hope for what she calls the "predicament of irreversibility" which is produced by the modern obscurantism of human ability and production. Something must be presented that is not tied to the order of things so that true love and freedom might enter into the hopeless and lonely existence of modernity.

[13] I am indebted to Simon Tugwell for the phrase and idea of forgiveness as an "incursion of the life of God in the world." See his remarkable book *Prayer: Living with God,* (Springfield IL: Templegate Publishers, 1980), 86.

[14] I am not arguing here for a separation of forgiveness from regeneration. They occur simultaneously in the believer's heart. We must be able to think about them in distinction however. The supernatural work of God is that which is done 'for' us in pardon. I am focusing attention here on the possible reasons for the remarkable occurrence of the term in creedal statements. Example of the pervasiveness of the use of the word forgiveness (or remission) probably patterned on the Old Roman Symbol which was the foundation of the Apostle's Creed. See the divine liturgy for the Eastern Church in St Chrysostom almost always following the goal of perfection in as the work of salvation the next concept is the initiating action of God's pardon (*aphesis*); pp. 15-16, 19, 21, 22, 26, 27, 31, 40, 41. *The Divine Liturgy of Saint John Chrysostom* (Brookline, Mass. Holy Cross Orthodox Press, 1985).

So shall my heavenly Father also do to you if each of you does not forgive his brother from your heart.

Matthew 18:35

8

Forgiveness From the Heart

THE ONLY REASON FOR FORGIVENESS

Jesus is always moving us toward the Cross. The Cross was the ultimate act of forgiveness, but He did more than forgive there. He died to change me. He died not only to meet my needs; He died to provide for me His life in me. That is why Jesus says the seemingly impossible: *Unless you forgive your brother from your heart, then these horrible things will happen to you because you've chosen that kind of life.*

Something must happen at the deepest level of my heart. The only reason for forgiveness is to make us holy. That is what Peter needed. His total focus was himself. That is what anyone needs who thinks they can "strangle" the ones nearest them with retributive rage. Without a Spirit-filled life all we have are years filled with resentments, tattered black books, and a train of broken-relationships we keep in a file cabinet in our souls entitled, "Justified Rejections." It may slip by us but Jesus shifts the pronouns to include all of us. It may seem as if the rest of Matthew 18 is directed to Peter but Jesus uses the plural 'you' twice in verse 35. All are accountable to "forgive your brother from your heart". The refusal to do so entails the gravest of consequences.[1]

Our Ability to Miss the Point

I am convinced that most of us misunderstand holiness. You may have a background in a tradition in which holiness meant a certain kind of worship or a certain kind of activity. Sadly, for the majority of us the concepts surrounding holiness are primarily negative rather than thrilling. The emphasis in this book is on a biblical conception of holiness, and not simply an historical expression. We are looking at the Holy One in an attempt to understand all we can about Him, and making appropriate personal responses as a result.

The holiness that Jesus is offering here is the Life of God in the soul of every believer and, thereby, the offer of the Life of God to the world. It is a conundrum to me how often I hear strong calls from Christian leaders to live according to the dictates of Scripture which are then followed by calls with a schizophrenic reserve on the possibility of living at that level. *Be holy…but we all know that's not possible so just try as hard as you can.*

Without a shadow of a doubt I know that is not what Jesus said, ever. He surely is not saying to Peter and the disciples, "Be as humble as you can on your own power; we all know you will cause some to stumble but try to keep that number to a minimum. Oh, and since we know that realistically it is impossible to forgive without number, count this as just an ideal I am throwing out there. I will add the notion of unremitting judgment if you don't forgive as an encouragement to try a bit harder!"

Jesus does give efficient grace for fulfilling all of His invitations to live His Life. His commandments are based upon His full provision for us and enablement to obediently respond. He also warns us that this Life is not a game. It is not something we can dictate by our experiences or understanding. All of it is beyond our doing. We need Him to *be* our Forgiveness and the Forgiveness we offer.

A Unique View of the Father

It seems we have been affected by Marcion's heresy for two millennia.[2] We have bought into the lie that the God of the Bible is divisible by our conceptions of graciousness. The Old Testament is full of a mean God, Yahweh; while the sensitive, understanding God is found in Jesus in the New Testament. One is "unpleasable"; the Other pleads to be accepted. Apparently Jesus did not get that memo. For in this chapter alone one finds that Jesus is as demanding, exacting and gracious as the Father.[3] The essence of the Trinity is clarified in the ministry of Jesus, not obscured. Jesus is not the politically-correct version of deity. He reveals the heart of the Father by the power of the Spirit.

We somehow miss the recurrent refrain of the seriousness of relational health in the mind of the Holy One.

If you cause one weaker in faith to sin – "it would be better for (you) to have a millstone hung around (your) neck and to be drowned in the depths of the sea" (18:6).

If you cause others to sin by the use of one of your members – "It is better for you to enter life maimed or crippled than to have two hands and two feet and be thrown into eternal fire" (18:8-9).

If you think a wandering soul is of no consequence, take another look at the Father's unending concern for the wayward one - "(Y)our Father in heaven is not willing that any of these little ones should be lost" (18:14)

And then there is this comment which is the last thing specifically said about the character of the Father before the Passion begins.

If you do not forgive your brother from your heart – "This is how my Father will treat each of you" (18:35). How? Verse 34 gives the outline. "In anger his master turned him over to the jailers (literally *torturers*) to be tortured, until he should pay back what he owes."

Apparently this is not a fireside chat that can be forgotten with the waning strains of Kumbaya. Jesus is laying out a non-negotiable principle. You must be forgiven. If you truly are under the cascade of redemptive grace, you will dispense that blessing to everyone with whom you come in contact. Our forgiveness toward others is but a faint echo of the ministry of the Trinity in our lives, but it must sound forth nonetheless. If it does not – according to Jesus, the consequences will be catastrophic. If you are not a recipient of mercy and if you are not transformed by that gift, you remove yourself from all the blessings of that mercy. The Triune One is exacting and empowering at the same time.

We should not say that Jesus is trying to scare us into forgiveness. That would be an odd view of holiness at best. What He is doing is laying down the foundations of how His life enters ours. Forgiveness is not an option. It is the essential entryway through which all of us begin to share in the divine self-giving. But forgiveness is only the beginning. The end of this work is that the servant would have a heart like His Master's. Functional, mechanical, reserved, portioned, self-focused forgiveness may be a humanly contrived contract but it has nothing to do with the heart that Jesus longs to produce in us.

All too often our theology culminates just at the point where Jesus' begins. We are satisfied with a release from the consequences of sins, and all the while He is offering freedom from that which produces sin. It is very hard to grab a twenty-five dollar debt receipt when an avalanche of grace is continually pouring into and out of one's heart and life. But if we have not comprehended grace then we will not give it, and that is not acceptable to the Father, or the Son, or the Holy Spirit.

Is Forgiving Works Righteousness?

We spoke earlier of how difficult it is to fully comprehend the grandeur of grace. That may be why we misinterpret the commands of Jesus to forgive. The only portion of the Lord's Prayer that has any commentary is that which pertains to forgiveness. Jesus has already interjected the only comparison in His entire model prayer, Forgive us our debts, as we also have forgiven our debtors (Mt 6:12). Then the series of petitions ends with an almost disconnected explanation, *For if you forgive men, when they sin against you, your heavenly Father will also forgive you. But if you do not forgive men their sins, your Father will not forgive your sins (Mt 6:14-15).*

If we are absolutely honest these verses seem, at first flush, to go against everything our modern doctrine of grace propounds. He is sovereign; He dispenses grace to whom He wills. If I am one of the fortunate ones, I am "in." But Jesus is never restricted within our syllogisms. They are far too mechanical and impersonal for the Son of the Father's Love.

That "as" in the middle of the petition is a key. *Forgive us our debts, as we also have forgiven our debtors.* We could translate it as a causative preposition. So that our forgiveness is a sort of dam, that when released enables God's grace to reach us. But that is fallacious because everything redemptive starts first in the heart of God. I don't make Him do anything by anything I do. Maybe the "as" is better understood as a comparative; He forgives and I want to model my life like His. That thought is true, but it does not carry just a simple lackadaisical comparison. Jesus does not come back to a petition for this universal prayer for mere light reflection. This is something He does not want anyone to miss. To try to circumvent this relationship is to miss salvation at its very source.

The "as" is a deeply relational term. It is similar to the other times that Jesus uses the same preposition in shocking ways. Matthew 5:48 may be the supreme example of all, "Be perfect, therefore, __as__ your heavenly Father is perfect." Paul adds his application of this theme where he writes, "Forgive __as__ the Lord forgave you" (Col 3:13). The sober Christian will feel rightfully overwhelmed by such commands – unless the relationship between Source and Receiver is clearly worked out.

Jesus would never say, "Do this work and then you will be saved." That is both pagan and non-Christian. What He is communicating is the nature of all salvation. To know Him is a constant receptivity of forgiving and thus, His transforming grace will naturally flow into all human relationships at all times. The moment we stop receiving, we stop giving truly. We are not "copying" God as Christians. That form of holiness kills life. The life of holiness Jesus offers is one of deep, intimate abiding in Him. (John 15)

We have noted how important context is in interpreting the meaning of any text. Is it at all surprising that Jesus is challenged by the most self-righteous religious prigs in Israel in the following paragraph along the lines of divorce (Matthew 19:1-9)? In the midst of a modern world awash in the cultural demise that accompanies the loosening of every familial responsibility, we need to hear what Jesus says about the constant need of forgiveness. It is no wonder that in the center of His debate with the legalists, Jesus comes back to the heart. He states that it was due to the 'hardness of heart" that divorce became allowable. Any married person who does not hear what Jesus says about forgiveness will live in constant tension. If married persons are not changed at the heart level they will act just like this wicked servant toward one another.

Imaging the Heart of God

What we are in relation to the Triune God is the very image of God (Gen 1:26; Col 3:10). We image His Life. That is not a reflection separate from the Light which illuminates. We image Him. Jesus is the Image of God. We are made in His Image. He is Forgiveness. We are forgiven. He must forgive through our lives. It is that last point which we don't like.

It is much more antiseptic to have Jesus be the One who gets involved with all the stuff we call sin. But He will never allow only that. We walk out of the courtroom free of a billion dollar debt for one purpose - to allow that amazing grace to flow to the ends of the earth beginning with the person who owes us. The immediacy of the life of grace is measured by the amount of time it takes for a believer to think, *either 'retribution' or 'forgiveness'*. That is the connection between His forgiving and ours. We don't earn salvation. We dispense it with lavish prodigality. We live in Him, and thus therefore "as" Him. Jesus never lives in an unreal place. His forgiveness is revealed and found in flesh and blood and soul. He wants to see that we are like Him, that we desire to be truly remade in His image.

That being said, we need to comprehend the absolutely critical nature of the human side of forgiveness. Having realized that all salvation flows from the unstinting holy love of the Triune God, it is remarkable that, in essence, the reserve of one human heart to another in forgiveness can obstruct the flow of uncircumscribable grace. Hannah Arendt's insightful comments are a shock to those in the Church who glibly attribute all to God, and leave human responsibility dangling without purpose. She writes,

> *First, it is not true that only God has the power to forgive, and second that this power does not derive from God – as though God, not men, would forgive through the medium of human beings – but on the contrary must be mobilized by men toward each other before they can hope to be forgiven by God also.*[4]

She is taking Jesus at his exact, non-equivocating word. He says
to us, "You must forgive from the heart if you expect to be forgiven at all."
This is not working one's way to God; it is God working His life out in us.

Whatever the metaphysics of that statement, the bottom line
is that we must absorb the pain of the sin done to us. That is a form of
death to self. The difficulty of that is resonant with the work of the Cross
as it reveals the agony of God who took into Himself our pain. This is
not a form of works; it is revelatory of the very nature of God in this
broken world. Jesus has never softened that call to "take up your cross
and follow me." Could it be that the first place a true disciple of Jesus
reveals the Master's essential nature is in the self-deferring love resident in
forgiveness?

Perhaps it is not an intrusion into the text to read "seventy
times seven" as a statement of optimistic joy rather than a grueling,
life-squelching command. What if instead of our normal interpretation
of a sober requirement that is only possible in the super-spiritual or
naïve 'doormat' theology of some, Jesus is offering exuberant freedom?
Sabbath (Hebrew "*Shabbat*" for 'rest' and "*sheva*" for "seven") might be a
significant undercurrent that we miss. Jesus offers rest and fulfillment that
are to be announced every time God's people come together for worship
every seven days.[5] The context where forgiveness ought to be the most
permeating is in the experience of Christian fellowship.

Jesus never invokes burdens. We make the relationship of
forgiveness something it was never meant to be. He intends it to bring
rest for the sin-weary, palpable victory, and powerful love. I return to the
point that the major creeds of the Church have chosen 'forgiveness' as the
salvific term to be spoken in the community of faith.[6] Is there a reason the
ancient Christians felt it was important to intone that term every time the
church proclaimed its central beliefs and life commitments?

Forgiveness from the Heart

The purpose of salvation is holiness of heart and life. All of Scripture confirms that the Holy One wants to share His nature with His beloved. The essence of God's own heart is Holy Love and that is what is birthed in believers when they are born again. The essence of both divine and human personhood is to be pure. The heart is the center of the person. Our heart is what defines us as a person. What comes out of that heart cannot be hidden (Mt. 12:34; 15:18-19). I might be able to lie to another human being and pretend to bear fruit, but the root issue of who I am will ultimately produce that which is external.

Jesus is never satisfied with a half-salvation. In fact, in Him there is no such thing. We are the ones who dare to divide up His atoning and sanctifying grace. To settle for less than the full implications of forgiveness is ignorance at best and defiance at worst. He will allow no diminishment of the work of the Cross and the power of the Resurrection.

What Jesus wanted for Peter and wants for us is a heart that is His to form and to fill. To forgive from the heart is another way of saying that He can do in us, if we are willing, that which looks like Him in everyday life. That is where He wants to show up. That is where all we say meets with the abrupt realization of demanding reality. The Savior delighted to interconnect with what we could offer in our brokenness. He offered restoring forgiveness. Now, He turns and invites us to join Him in the same motivation for life.

Matthew 18 has been the center of our discussion and we must keep the purposes of God in mind. We have seen that forgiveness can easily be turned into a form of religious ethics without really being the result of a dynamic relationship with God. A renunciation of the gift of God's release from sin produces mayhem interpersonally and intra-personally. The unspoken center of the whole parable that comes on the heels of Peter's revealing question is the heart. The heart of compassion in the Master is the pivotal issue in the story of each of us. To not forgive as we are forgiven is a heart problem; first in reception and then in transmission.

So it ought not to surprise us that the climax of this transitional chapter in the life of the Master and His disciples deals with the heart. Jesus' righteous wrath is reflected in the identical just response of the Father (18:35). But Jesus also brings Peter (and us by unmistakable implication) to the beginning point. Peter had asked about forgiving his brother. After all that is required and illustrated, there is no soft close. Jesus gets just about as radical as we will ever find Him to be. You walk right into the judgment of your choice and God's holy wrath if you do not forgive your brother from your heart.

"From your heart," then puts all of us under the unerring microscope of the Holy Spirit's incisive discernment. If there are numbers games, little black books, unresolved resentments, unreceptive spirits, and hardened hearts, then we get exactly what we have asked for – torment.[7] But if the absolute remission of the debt of guilt, shame, and all the ramifications of our sin are thrown upon the heart of the Savior and removed from us, then our heart should be a channel of an outflow of grace which first meets the 'brother' or the 'other' with forgiveness.

Holy love must image itself in us. Compassion for the sinner issues out of the Spirit-poured love that must fill a heart in order for forgiveness to be more than mere politics. The access which the Holy Spirit wants to have in a believer's entire life can be stunted if a lack of forgiveness pervades. That is why Jesus can start out His basic discipleship program with the fundamental of forgiveness. Those who have gone on to explore the Spirit-filled life are enjoined to forgive even as Christ has forgiven them. There will never be a time, this side of heaven, when a believer will get past the need to forgive.

No one who has given themselves to the focus of this book should leave it without asking this question "Is my heart filled with the forgiving

love of God?" There is no way to forgive truly and continually without
that deeper reality. Jesus never said that forgiveness was all we need. He
knew the deeper needs of our hearts, but He insisted on dealing with all
the barriers that could keep a person from receiving the fullness for which
forgiveness prepares. Imputation offered for us by grace in salvation must
always issue into the impartation of that grace within the heart (see chart).
Forgiveness without the inner cleansing of the heart is not the Gospel; it is
a faint shadow of the glorious freedom of the children of God.

Imputation	Impartation
What God does for us	What God does in us
External	Internal
Objective	Subjective
Judicial	Personal
Rightness before God	Union with God
Emphasis on Satisfaction through Atonement	Emphasis on Transformation through the Presence of the Holy Spirit
Forgivness	New Birth

Forgiveness, with its counterpart, the new birth, is offered as the
promise of the complete sanctifying work of God. The incursion of the Life
of God must be received, and that is the actual personal presence of the
Holy Spirit. Forgiveness is nothing less than the invitation into the very life
of God. Thus, forgiveness without the cleansing of the heart would not be
sufficient to meet the needs of all believers. Oswald Chambers, renowned
for his uncanny ability to speak theologically across the normal divisive
lines, writes, "When God forgives a man, He not only alters him but
transmutes what he has already done. Forgiveness does not mean merely
that I am saved from sin and made right for heaven; forgiveness means
that I am forgiven into a recreated relationship to God."[8]

The heart indicates the essence of a person. Nothing could be clearer than that the steward misunderstood grace. Even though forgiven, he did not receive forgiveness. His heart, unable to forgive, revealed the lack of what Jesus said His Father most wanted - a heart overflowing with the holy love of God. Instead of the relationship of freedom and acceptance with another person that God offered, he was left with the torture of "unreceived" compassion and "ungiving" pardon.

Jesus has so much more for us than we can ever comprehend. He is not fixing us up or patching over our junk. He is after a complete restoration of the image He has created. He wants us to have His mind, His disposition. Chambers underscores this: "Forgiveness means not merely that I am saved from hell and made right for heaven (no man would accept forgiveness on such a level); forgiveness means that I am forgiven into a recreated relationship, into identification with God in Christ. The miracle of Redemption is that God turns me, the unholy one, into the standard of Himself, the Holy One, by putting into me a new disposition, the disposition of Jesus Christ."[9] To forgive as *Christ has forgiven us* means that something has been transfused, transmitted, and appropriated in my life, through which my responses to sin committed against me are fully grounded in the cleansing work of the Holy Spirit. All forgiveness starts from the heart of God but His method includes a heart that is freed from every form of sinful self-protection. When that work occurs then true forgiveness from a human heart can both mirror the love of God and become a conduit for that holy love to another. May it be.

---

1 Wesley, among other previous commentators, uses Mt 18:34-35 as one of the clearest references to hell and damnation used by Jesus. Wesley is definitely not mincing words when he connects damnation with unforgiveness. See example *The Works of John Wesley* XIII:434.

2 Marcion was a bishop in Sinope (an area of modern day Turkey once called Pontus) ca. 85-160AD.

3 "Beware of the pleasant view of the Fatherhood of God—God is so kind and loving that of course He will forgive us. That sentiment has no place whatever in the New Testament. The only ground on which God can forgive us is the tremendous tragedy of the Cross of Christ; to put forgiveness on any other ground is unconscious blasphemy. The only ground on which God can forgive sin and reinstate us in His favour is through the Cross of Christ, and in no other way. Forgiveness, which is so easy for us to accept, cost the agony of Calvary. It is possible to take the forgiveness of sin, the gift of the Holy Ghost, and our sanctification with the simplicity of faith, and to forget at what enormous cost to God it was all made ours."
Oswald Chambers, *My Utmost for His Highest*, Nov. 20.

4 Arendt, *The Human Condition*, 215.

5 *Theological Wordbook of the Old Testament*, II:898.

6 This point has been made at least three times in previous chapters.

7 The word for torture (*basanistes*) is found in this form only in Matthew. It comes from the root *basanizo* that refers to the physical distresses that torment (Mt 8:6), the distress on the spirit brought on by others sins (2 Pet. 2:8) and the future torments of the hell and the eschaton from both God and from His defeated foes (Lk 16:23, Rev 9:5; 14:10; 20:10; the book of Revelation has the most references to torment than any other book of the NT.

8 Oswald Chambers, *The Place of Help*

9 *Ibid., My Utmost for His Highest*, Nov 19.

> *Truly I say to you, whatever you shall bind on earth shall be bound in heaven; and whatever you loose on earth shall be loosed in heaven. Again I say to you, that if two of you agree on earth about anything that they may ask, it shall be done for them by My Father who is in heaven. For where two or three have gathered together in My name, there I am in their midst.*
> Matthew 18:35

9

Forgiving As Christ

The unforgivingness [of] our neighbor; the shutting of him out from the
mercies, from our love –so from the universe, as far as we are a portion
of it [is], the murdering therefore of our neighbor. It may be an infinitely
less evil to murder a man than to refuse to forgive him. The former may
be the act of a moment of passion: the latter is the heart's choice. It is
spiritual murder, the worst, to hate, to brood over the feeling that
excludes, that kills the image, the idea of the hated.
George MacDonald, *"It Shall Not be Forgiven"*

A PERSONAL DEFINITION OF FORGIVENESS

It is difficult to summarize, much less define, a major biblical
theme. Defining forgiveness is comparable to defining love or holiness.
The task ought not to be approached cavalierly. Every point of theology,
when reflected upon for any length of time, is comparable to trying
to explain a vast ocean of truth or a mountain vista of reality. Words
seem so inadequate. Merely rational explanations must bow before the

incredible mystery to which they can only point. That is one reason why Jesus spoke in parables. Pictures of common economic affairs, as in the parable of the forgiving master and the unforgiving servant, bear eternal realities which resist narrow interpretations.

But Jesus never solely offered information. His method of teaching always required a response of heart and life. People are created to respond to truth either by reception or rejection. Every one of His remarkable metaphors of reality which are encapsulated in real-life scenarios requires the inquiring heart to do something. And that responsiveness must be deeper than the previous engagement.[1] The center of our discussion is the parable that deals with forgiveness in increasing intensity. Peter's question (Mt 18:21) is representative of all of us. We want to know when the retribution can begin while retaining some modicum of civility. Jesus' reply is not what Peter (or we) ever expected.

Underlying all that has been said is the belief that the depersonalizing effects of sin can be transformed by the recreating nature of God's Life. His Life is a Triune one, the only true personal Life. When that essence is offered and received by faith all impersonal notions of redemption pale in significance. John and Charles Wesley often corrected the Protestant Reformation's tendency to over-emphasize the experience of pardon. That lopsided emphasis individualizes forgiving grace, rather than revealing the personal, relational and transforming qualities of forgiveness. Charles Wesley wrote often of the goal of forgiveness,

He deigns in flesh to appear,
Widest extremes to join;
To bring our vileness near,
And make us all divine:
And we the life of God shall know,
For God is manifest below.[2]

Pardon from sin occurs as the self-giving God fills the penitent heart with Himself. The more explicit theological analysis is that forgiveness and regeneration occur "concomitantly" or simultaneously. That is, they are distinguishable ideas but they actually occur at the same time and are inseparable. To leave either aspect out is to miss something of the fullness of personal salvation. As we have recounted, the servant who did not receive the personal gift offered to him by the compassionate heart of his lord, could not see himself or his colleague as fully personal. To remain in legality alone and to reduce relationships to stark economic restitution depersonalizes, and that means that there is no true personal giving possible. To forgive is to love the unlovable. A full personal love is only possible between persons, not entities.

My deepest concern is that Christians seem to be quite at ease with limiting the power of pardon to a legal transaction in the mind or will of God. Rather than focusing on the cost behind forgiveness, the personal self-offering for another's sake, we have forced ourselves into a corner. In the hopes that we are not seen as adding too much to the human side of salvation, we have mistakenly portrayed a God who clears our sinful accounts but then leaves us to work the rest out on our own. When that happens is that forgiveness becomes a numbers game, a weathered black book, a 'mercantilistic' negotiation. This parable, as Jesus intended it, brings the reality of forgiveness straight to our hearts and forces us to look at the greatness of our Savior's pardon and our deep need of His recreative work. To forgive from the heart, to forgive as God in Christ has forgiven us, requires nothing less than the third Person of the Trinity in all of His power to be present in our lives.

Three Definitive Elements[3]

The three recurring definitive elements which direct the mind, the heart and the will to the mystery and beauty of forgiveness are:

1. *Process* – Forgiveness is never solely a commitment of the will in a moment. To ignore sin is not a moral option. True forgiveness incorporates the realization that a relationship has been so damaged that only grace can resurrect it. The time needed for a full revelation of the grace of God in dealing with sin, ours or sin done against us, begins in a moment of decision, but the necessity of the on-going influence of that pardon includes a process. Another important consideration is that forgiveness is never an end in itself. The beauty in this discovery of the heart of God is that it opens up new possibilities of freedom from shame, guilt and decimation of relationship.

2. *Bearing* – Though there are many symbols and metaphors which help to capture the depth of forgiveness, the idea of bearing another within one's own heart is quite possibly the most helpful in trying to comprehend both divine and human forgiveness. As mentioned above, the mystery of forgiveness requires more from us than superficial readings of reality.

Seen from the foundation upon which all legal (pardon) and mercantile (debt) images are built, there must be the absorption of another's sin into the heart of the one sinned against. If no one suffers there is no forgiveness. Any other attempt at dispensing with sin is absolutely inadequate until the Cross is brought into the middle of the brokenness. It is not God's love alone that pardons us. Holiness demands an atonement for sin. If God forgave us without bearing our sin on the Cross, He would be complicit in our sin. Likewise, anyone who forgives a brother or sister will identify with the work of the Savior to such an extent that they will carry the offender in their heart and not give to them what they rightfully deserve. (Perhaps this is pertains to the cross that Jesus tells us His disciples will carry daily.)

3. *Openness* – Christian forgiveness, the kind that is experienced in personal redemption, is always relational. We have learned that God is always open to a restoration of relationship. In evangelical Christianity we have come to the point of presuming upon God in this regard. We act as if we may sin with impunity and then virtually demand that He forgive us. In a warped manner we try to bring God in on our prescribed doctrine of salvation. He states He loves us; the argument goes, so that requires that He take us back into relationship every time we plead forgiveness. God is not mocked, however, nor is His salvation to be trivialized. While God is open to a restoration of intimacy with us through forgiving grace, there are standards of continued growth. He forgives persons who have sinned and He does not stop with mere transactions. He is not reducible to our cramped notions of judicial performance.

Likewise, those who forgive in Christ's name are willing to begin the Spirit-led possibility of restoring a relationship with the wrong-doer. There are too many examples of those who have forgiven as Christ has, who have brought horrendous sinners back into their lives after the offense has been dealt with, for us to negate the same possibility in all of our lives. God does not repel anyone who shows Him a sincere desire for a transformed relationship. Therefore, there is no warrant for volitional rejection of a penitent sinner within the New Testament at any moral level.

Paying the Price as Christ

Each of these three points has been explored in this book. While the ideas contained in this book are not exhaustive, they clearly point to crucial steps toward forgiveness. We need to allow the Spirit of Christ to glorify the Father through our daily forgiveness of real people in stark, real time and space. Before any reservation, boundaries or excuses are cast up at various levels, we must allow the Triune God to form our hearts, and our responses to sin committed against us. The heart which has truly experienced the full release from all sin will be so malleable to the working of the Spirit that there will be a disposition like that of Jesus. Forgiveness begins first in the heart of the one wronged. It is a willingness to take the sinner into the heart. The self dies when forgiveness truly occurs. We are commanded to forgive as Christ (Mt 6:12,14-15; 18:35; Col 3:13; Eph 4:32). "Take up your cross, deny yourself..."

In our day with the media casting horrors before us hourly, it is quite easy to settle for an analysis of wrongs by justice alone. On a Christian news website I read a string of responses to the killing of Kenyan Christians by Somalian Muslim terrorists. The line of argumentation, which no one challenged, was: if they kill one of us (Christians) it ought to be that ten thousand of them should die. As I read that I thought of the Nigerian bishop participating in a class I was teaching in Lagos who asked me a searing question about a similar scenario in his own family life. He was visibly distraught as he asked, "What would you do if your cousin had been dragged out of his house and had a tire filled with gasoline placed around his neck and then had been set afire by the Muslims?" There is a God-given rage and cry for justice in all of us in light of such atrocities. Is that kind of terror forgivable?

I have had the privilege of preaching on the radio for eighteen years. No series I have ever preached has garnered the kind of responses that a month long discussion of forgiveness did. Most of the correspondence pertained to incredible suffering and the desire to know a proper Christian response. A campmeeting that often asks me to come and share offers a workshop for the adults in the mornings. I had been there at least five times before without much reaction to anything I taught in that workshop. But the year we covered forgiveness, when we discussed requirements of actual forgiveness, several of the men confronted me with anger in their voice and posture. They found that notion of forgiving just as Christ does extremely difficult to imbibe and to apply.

Nearly every time I have shared concerning a full-orbed biblical doctrine of forgiveness, someone has responded with something along the line of, "Well, apparently you have not suffered like I have!" That sentiment, when interpreted, often means, "I have every right to retain rage and the refusal to ever deal with that person again." I have felt the pressure to concede because the stories I hear are heart-breaking. I have felt the anger rise in my own being against the abuse, the self-exalting damage spewed by seemingly animal-like persons. But, if God was in Christ reconciling the world to Himself when I was complicit in the death of God, and He offered to take me back, then how do I truly show that Heart to those around me? It has to start with the willingness to begin a process of bearing another in my own heart. And from that Cross-stamped choice I have to be open to the Holy Spirit guiding me into what He wants in terms of restoration or reconciliation.

In the final days of writing this book I came across a video of a mother who had forgiven the man who had senselessly murdered her daughter. Typically beneath the video was the choice to 'like' or 'dislike' the message. I was not surprised to find a large number of rejections and a very minute number of agreements with what the mother had done. I would like to have been able to read the responses of those who thought the mother was naïve, stupid, dishonoring of her daughter's life. I have wanted to know how that precious woman replies to those who consider what she has done to be utterly ridiculous or even immoral. I wonder what she would say to Simon Wiesenthal. She has a right to speak to those who have suffered that I do not have. I cannot say that I know fully what is right in that kind of life-shaking situation. All I can say is that there, right there in the face and heart of that mother of a murdered child, is something like the heart of the Father of the Son that only the Holy Spirit can produce in the process of bearing a sinner in one's own being.

The man who committed that murder did go to prison. But the victim's mother went and visited the guilty man. It was not long before she told him of the true reason for her visits, and through the Plexiglas partition forgave him. She consistently offered him the grace of Jesus. When he was released after serving his time, she adopted him into her life like a son, guiding, challenging, investing, and expecting personal responsibility. His testimony revealed the stabilizing effect of the grace of God poured into his life through the channel of the mother of the daughter he had senselessly murdered. It would have been possible for him to take advantage of her gracious behavior. There are endless possibilities for the human heart to lie to itself and to all around. But, there is the much more hopeful, grace-filled possibility that sin does not have the last word, and that forgiveness is not some cheap, sentimental ornament. That hope resides at the very center of who Jesus is, why He came and what He desires to restore in every person who has sincerely cried out, "Jesus, forgive me a sinner."

Some who have read this book have offered their frank assessment. They have lovingly said that I am not being realistic enough, that I have made forgiveness sound too easy, that I am more of a mystic than a practical theologian. They are probably all correct. However, I do want to live merely as one who has been forgiven much and loves because of that remitted debt. I want to learn what it means to allow the Holy Spirit to assist me in seeing the deepest need of my own heart if I de-personalize the wrongdoer. I want to be as Christ in pouring out my heart in love, in taking the offender into my heart. As Christ took

our judgment into Himself, we must be like him in the orientation of
our heart. He bore us in His sinless heart, though we are deeply flawed
by the Fall. The judgment inherent in grace must allow grace to shed
its light on every person involved in a sinful act. We must accept all
personal responsibility in the chaos and offer hope by not giving the
retributive justice the other might deserve.[4] This can only be done if the
Spirit of Christ so fills our hearts that we invite His honest appraisal of
the reality of the entire situation.

To forgive as Christ is to do so without any air of condescension.
There is no forgiveness between two persons that is mere transaction.
Just like any virtue, forgiveness is most often mundane, boring,
and unheralded. It is plain, hard, real life in Christ which is seldom
scintillating. Most of us will forgive all of our lives without anyone
offering medals or sainthood.[5] It is a stark, humbling, earthy thing that
Christ can fill with His resurrection reality. The forgiver, the bearer, must
know their standing in Christ and say, "I am here, I am the one who
has received this wrong, but I am the one who must allow Jesus to deal
with it in me." The forgiver then becomes, "as Christ". This is no more
mystical than dying with Christ or being raised with Him. It is not one
whit less real than being hidden with God in Christ. Apart from Him
we are not forgiven and we can forgive no one. Apart from Holy Love
poured into our hearts by the blessed Holy Spirit all we have left is
our own self-produced, dressed-up negotiations that resemble the real
inescapable 'tormentors' at the end of the parable (Mt 18:34).

We have to live as Christ, which means He has to live His Life in
us. That is always His desire. The "as" in, "forgiving as Christ", depends
upon our receptivity of the continually deepening flow of the Love
which the Triune Persons mutually share. Forgiveness from the heart
is not a motto by which to feel better about one's self. It is a dynamic
fullness which can only be given from above, a divine dispensation. As

a theologian from the Eastern Church states, Even the remission of sins is brought about because when we "co-habit" with God, the ocean of divine goodness annihilates human sins. In its full reality forgiveness is "communion with Christ" and "communion with the Kingdom of Christ."[6]

Imaging the heart of Christ has to move from creed to community. Just as forgiveness can be seen as the point of incursion of the life of God in the world, it is also the place where true Christian fellowship begins and is maintained.[7] The Lord's Prayer is meant to be a communal act as the plural pronouns "us" and "you" clearly indicate.[8] No one is above repentance. No one ceases to need forgiveness.[9] We recognize the inseparable nature of the mutual forgiving love of the Body of Christ from its source in the Father, Son and Holy Spirit. To live in Christ is to join Him in His ministry. The ministry of bearing one another includes the good, the bad and the ugly. Forgiveness always means offering love where it is least deserved.[10] If the priests of the Temple ministry bore the needs of Israel upon their breasts, how much more will the Kingdom of priests that Jesus rules bear the sins of the people with Him.

---

[1] C.H. Dodd wrote, "At its simplest a parable is a metaphor or simile drawn from nature or common life, arresting the hearer by its vividness or strangeness, and leaving the mind in sufficient doubt about its precise application to tease it into active thought." *The Parables of the Kingdom* (New York: Charles Scribner's Sons, 1961) , 5.

[2] Nativity Hymns 1745 Hymn #5, verse 5, can be found at, https://www.google.com/url?q=http://divinity.duke.edu/sites/default/files/documents/cswt/31_Nativity_Hymns_(1745

[3] Much has been written of forgiveness. Some of the work has focused on interpersonal dynamics. Fewer have have striven to offer a fully Trinitarian doctrine of forgiveness without keeping practical issues at arm's length. The three elements of my "definition" of forgiveness are foundational themes which are, in essence, summaries of many works that I have delved into from the early church to the present.

[4] Jones, *Embodying Forgiveness*, 147 discusses the move from 'holding one accountable' to accepting responsibility.

[5] Williams, "(Forgiveness) will be very hard; it will also be very dull. Forgiveness is not normally a thrilling or exciting thing." *The Forgiveness of Sins*, 112.

[6] Panayiotis Nellas, *Deification in Christ* (Crestwood: St. Vladimir's Seminary Press, 1987),193.

[7] Bonhoeffer, *Cost of Discipleship*, 323.

[8] Bonhoeffer, *Cost of Discipleship*, 188.

[9] Williams clarifies this equality of responsibility, "Many reconciliations have unfortunately broken down because both parties have come prepared to forgive and unprepared to be forgiven." *The Forgiveness of Sins*, 113. What is remarkable about this appraisal is that it was written with the Nazis in mind in the era just after WWII. The difficult notions of cost, bearing and self-judgment begin to bore in deeply in a context of that volatility.

[10] George MacDonald, *Creation in Christ, ed. R. Hein* (Wheaton: Shaw Publishers, 1976), 51.